LIVING LIGHT

Conserving Bioluminescent Plants and Animals

STEPHEN AITKEN

ORCA BOOK PUBLISHERS

Published in Canada and the United States in 2024
by Orca Book Publishers.
orcabook.com

Library and Archives Canada Cataloguing in Publication
Title: Living light : conserving bioluminescent
plants and animals / Stephen Aitken.
Names: Aitken, Stephen, 1953- author.
Series: Orca wild ; 14.
Description: Series statement: Orca wild ; 14 |
Includes bibliographical references and index.
Identifiers: Canadiana (print) 2023058215X | Canadiana
(ebook) 2023058268 | ISBN 9781459837294
(hardcover) | ISBN 9781459837300 (PDF)
| ISBN 9781459837317 (EPUB)
Subjects: LCSH: Bioluminescence—Juvenile literature.
| LCSH: Wildlife conservation—Juvenile
literature. | LCSH: Plant conservation—Juvenile
literature. | LCGFT: Informational works. |
LCGFT: Instructional and educational works.
Classification: LCC QH641 .A38 2024 | DDC j572/.4358—dc23

Library of Congress Control Number: 2023949576

Summary: Part of the nonfiction Orca Wild series for middle-grade readers and illustrated with color photographs throughout, this book examines the biology, habitat and environmental threats facing bioluminescent species on land and in the water.

Orca Book Publishers gratefully acknowledges the support for its publishing programs provided by the following agencies: the Government of Canada, the Canada Council for the Arts and the Province of British Columbia through the BC Arts Council and the Book Publishing Tax Credit.

Front cover photo(s) by GaryKavanagh/Getty Images
Back cover photo by Chasing Light/Getty Images
Author photo by Reta Mae Zelikovitz
Design by Troy Cunningham
Edited by Kirstie Hudson

Printed and bound in South Korea.

27   26   25   24   •   1   2   3   4

Japanese fireflies leave illuminated trails at night in a forest in Okayama, Japan.
JGALIONE/GETTY IMAGES

To the brave ones
who nurture the
light within.

CONTENTS

Sea fireflies are tiny crustaceans usually found in warm, tropical marine waters. They can also wash up on beach sands during low tide. Their luminous displays are best seen in areas of low light pollution.
TDUB VIDEO/GETTY IMAGES

INTRODUCTION

Imagine you're surrounded by darkness, not a light in sight. You can't even see the hand in front of your face. What would you do? You'd probably reach for a light switch, grab a flashlight or light the campfire. Animals don't have these options. Some very special species have responded to darkness in their habitat by evolving the ability to create their own light. These light makers are among the most spectacular wonders of the natural world. They use a language of light to communicate, to reproduce and to feed and defend themselves—they use light to survive!

An orange ocher glow is rising behind the distant blue misty hills as I type these words. Soon sunlight will wash across the river valley, backlight the mountain forests and splash across my keyboard. Light holds great power. A firefly in flight during the daytime is barely visible, but at night, with its back end lit up? It immediately demands attention.

Take an evening stroll through a grassy meadow studded with fireflies, linger on a luminous coastal beach with sparkling waters flowing between your toes, or huddle over the glow of foxfire mushrooms lighting up a forest floor. Witness for yourself one of nature's greatest superpowers.

BIOLUMINESCENCE

Bioluminescence (by-oh-loo-mih-NEH-sense) is light created and emitted by living organisms—*bios* means "life" in Greek, and *lumen* is Latin for "light." *Cold light*, as it is sometimes called, is remarkably efficient. A regular yellow (incandescent) light bulb loses 90 percent of its energy through heat, while bioluminescence hardly loses any. Light is energy. Plants use sunlight for *photosynthesis*, capturing its energy using only chlorophyll, carbon dioxide (CO_2) and water and releasing life-giving oxygen into the air. As magical as this process is, it dims in comparison to the wondrous organisms that create their own light.

The importance of this ability is highlighted by the fact that it arose so many times throughout evolution, in different species and with different chemistries.

FEEL THE MAGIC

In the past 50 years the study of bioluminescence, once considered a small side branch of biology, has grown into an important area of research. Many of the mysteries of how living organisms make light are starting to be unlocked. These unique processes are being developed into tools that have proven useful in medical and biological research laboratories around the world and have even inspired fine artists to create "living art." But we are in danger of losing many of these magical creatures almost as quickly as they are being studied and discovered.

It is more important than ever that precious ecosystems and the unique life they contain are conserved. We need to protect the vast oceans that harbor this rich biodiversity. Luminous marine creatures are vulnerable to plastic pollution, overfishing, deep-sea mining, and oil and gas explorations, among other threats. The ever-widening impacts of the climate crisis are taking their toll too—rising sea levels, ocean acidification, extreme weather patterns and increasing temperatures on land and in ocean waters. Bioluminescent organisms are threatened by light pollution, habitat loss and pesticides that devastate insect and *microbial* life.

I hope that as you read this book, you will come to see and feel the magic of these living light makers, and that more attention will be drawn to conserving them. There remain many mysteries hidden on our wonderful planet. Perhaps you'll be the one to unlock more of the secrets held by the light makers.

Fireflies light up a forest at night. These male beetles are using their yellow flashes to attract females.
TREVOR WILLIAMS/GETTY IMAGES

Bioluminescent mushrooms on a forest floor in Borneo emit a soft green glow.
ALEX FROOD/GETTY IMAGES

1
OUT OF
DARKNESS

> For [a] lucky few, bioluminescence is not one of nature's obscure and little-known oddities; it is one of their most precious and lasting memories.
>
> —from *Below the Edge of Darkness*, by Dr. Edith Widder

Luminous organisms have long inspired writers and poets. Tiny beetles flashing in the night can be an important reminder that it is the small, simple things in life that matter the most. Many haiku, a Japanese poetic form, have been written about fireflies, or "burning angels." Their flashing lights are sometimes considered to be the wandering souls of loved ones who have departed.

Come! Come! I call.
But the fireflies
Flash away into the darkness.
—HAIKU BY UEJIMA ONITSURA (1661–1738)

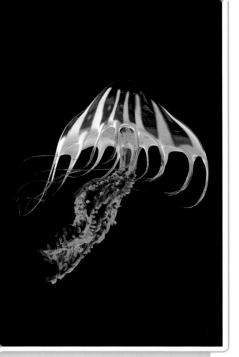

The reasons for emitting light can vary between jellyfish species: to attract prey, to camouflage their silhouettes against surface waters, to scare off predators or to communicate with other members of their species.
COREY FORD/STOCKTREK IMAGES/ GETTY IMAGES

OUR GLOWING PLANET

Creatures that make light have fascinated humankind for centuries. Pliny the Elder, a Roman philosopher and naturalist, walked the paths of ancient Rome at night with a glowing staff coated in the luminous secretions of jellyfish. Needless to say, his followers were impressed. The Batak people on the island of Palawan in the Philippines have taken a more practical approach. They carry glowing mushrooms to light their way through dark, misty rainforests. The tunnels of coal mines in the United Kingdom, where flames of any kind could cause an explosion of volatile gases, were once lit with dried luminescent fish skins.

SHINING EXAMPLE

More than half a billion years ago the first eyes evolved in animals. Bioluminescence showed up not long after. Now most animals have eyes, and they have become an almost indispensable tool for survival. Eyes have special pigments that translate the different frequencies of light into color. Bioluminescent organisms are special. They create their own light through unique chemicals made within their own bodies. On land bioluminescence is limited to a few insects and plants, but ocean waters are home to many more. The sheer volume of Earth's oceans, much of it at depths out of reach to sunlight, has resulted in not just billions or trillions of bioluminescent ocean creatures but quadrillions!

Bioluminescence has arisen over 40 different times throughout the evolution of life on Earth. Organisms that make their own light appear across a wide range of families in the animal kingdom, from insects to jellyfish to giant squid. Half of the known animal phyla (groupings of organisms with similar body plans), from microbes to vertebrates, contain luminous species. Bioluminescence is a shining example of convergent evolution, the appearance of similar body functions in many different branches of the evolutionary tree. Nature appears to have solved the same problem—how to survive in dark environments—over and over again in a wide range of ecosystems, from the sky to the ocean and deep in the earth.

IN THE AIR

I first encountered fireflies in the forest near my home outside Ottawa when I was seven years old. We called them lightning bugs. I still remember that twinkling magical night when the trees and stars danced together in a grassy field.

This scorpion fish (photographed under ultraviolet, or UV, light) is an example of a fluorescent marine species. It is not bioluminescent. Many marine animals are fluorescent, and new camera developments are allowing researchers to discover the remarkable ways that fluorescence helps the animals survive.
GIORDANO CIPRIANI/GETTY IMAGES

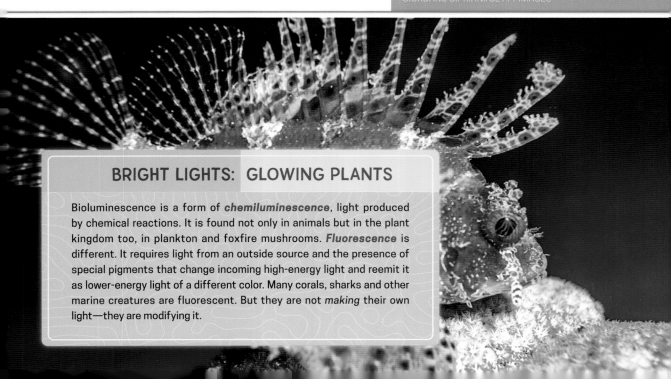

BRIGHT LIGHTS: GLOWING PLANTS

Bioluminescence is a form of *chemiluminescence*, light produced by chemical reactions. It is found not only in animals but in the plant kingdom too, in plankton and foxfire mushrooms. *Fluorescence* is different. It requires light from an outside source and the presence of special pigments that change incoming high-energy light and reemit it as lower-energy light of a different color. Many corals, sharks and other marine creatures are fluorescent. But they are not *making* their own light—they are modifying it.

A southern flying squirrel clings to a tree trunk in Michigan. This species looks brown under white light, but under ultraviolet light it reveals its secret—a fluorescent, bubblegum-pink body color.
LEE RENTZ/ALAMY STOCK PHOTO

Fireflies, which are actually beetles, are known by a lot of names, but some of my favorites are blinkies, fire beetles, candle flies and fire devils. They add sparkle to backyards, grassy lots, fields and forests on every continent except Antarctica (brrrr…too cold!). The male firefly signals a female of the same species with specially timed flashes of light, waiting for that special brilliant one to light up her own *abdomen* in response. There are over 2,000 species worldwide. In the United States and Canada alone, there are 160 different species. Sadly, more than 20 of those are threatened with extinction.

IN CAVES

Down under, in Australia and New Zealand, there are caves that could send a chill up any spine. (True confession: dark, wet underground caves creep me out.) At first glance these glowing caverns look like they're decked out for a festival, with hundreds of long strings of blue-green lights hanging from the ceiling. But a closer look reveals that the strings are actually threads of sticky glowing mucus made by gnat larvae. Unsuspecting prey are quickly paralyzed by chemicals in the guck. They get stuck to the luminous lines like flies to flypaper and are soon to become food for the hungry larvae. And the hungrier the larvae get, the brighter they glow!

IN THE SOIL

Railroad worms (which are actually beetle larvae) are commonly found in tropical soils, tucked into underground

burrows. If you're lucky, you might see them at night crawling up the trunks of trees. The female larva, only two inches (five centimeters) in length at full stretch, have 11 pairs of greenish yellow **photophores**, making them look like miniature passenger trains.

Winged males, with feather-like antennae, fly search patrols for females in the dark. You might mistake the larvae for millipedes, but closer inspection shows they have only six legs, not several hundred. In fact, millipedes are on the top of the railroad worm's menu of great things to eat. The greenish glow of these larvae sends a warning to predators: "Don't eat me. I'm toxic, and I taste terrible." Some Brazilian species have red headlights up front, giving them special night vision since their prey cannot see red.

ON THE FOREST FLOOR

The wild and wonderful world of **fungi** has evolved 70 luminous species that turn forest floors into magical fairy kingdoms. These glowing mushrooms have playful names like bitter oyster, little ping-pong bats, green pepe, lilac bonnet and—one of my personal favorites—the eternal light mushroom.

Bioluminescent larvae (inset) and their sticky threads hang from the roofs of New Zealand caves. The glowing lines attract and capture flies, mosquitoes, moths and even small snails and millipedes. The larval form lives for 6–12 months before turning into an adult fly.

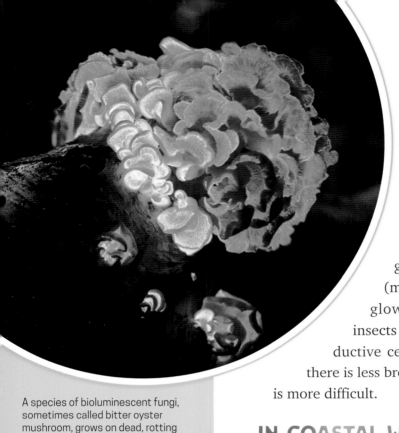

Green pepe is a common name given to glowing pale-green fungus that grows in subtropical Asia, including Australia and Brazil. The most impressive species have glowing mushroom caps, while others save their shine for their rootlike *mycelia* growing and glowing beneath the soil. Mycologists (mushroom scientists) believe that the glow of the mushroom caps attracts insects that help spread the spores (reproductive cells) thoughout forest floors, where there is less breeze and wind dispersal of the spores is more difficult.

A species of bioluminescent fungi, sometimes called bitter oyster mushroom, grows on dead, rotting wood. These mushrooms will grow in almost any hardwood forest in the world, as long as there are rotting branches, logs and stumps.
YLEM/WIKIMEDIA COMMONS/
PUBLIC DOMAIN

IN COASTAL WATERS

If you live near the ocean, you might have seen what you thought were fireflies in the water. They're actually sea fireflies (*ostracods*), tiny sea creatures that sparkle in water just like fireflies do in air but are not related to the glowing beetles found on land. After a tropical sunset on a moonless night, the males of these sesame-seed-sized organisms rise from their sandy coastal beds and spew out

The sandy beach on the coast of Okayama, Japan, sparkles with sea fireflies. The large coastal rocks serve as a dark canvas for the luminous blue fluids dripping from these tiny marine crustaceans.
TDUB_VIDEO/
GETTY IMAGES

light, creating silvery waters sprinkled with what appear to be strings of small stars. Females of the species move toward the dazzling light in a behavior not unlike the summer courtship rituals of fireflies on land.

Bioluminescent *dinoflagellates* (wow, big name!) are members of the plankton family. They create another glowing coastal phenomenon called sparkling seas. These microorganisms get their name from their whirling tails (*dino* means "whirling" in Greek, *flagellum* is Latin for "tail" or "whip"). Bioluminescent varieties of these single-celled creatures can produce a bluish-green light when stimulated by movement.

A deep-sea female anglerfish (appropriately called a black seadevil) carries its luminous lure over its head in a modified dorsal.
DOUG PERRINE/ALAMY STOCK PHOTO

When concentrations reach several million per gallon (3.8 liters) of water, they light up all at once, creating glowing blue beaches. Plankton feeders and other predators that enter the colony to feed are spotlighted like a jewelry-store thief caught in a security light. Most biologists believe that the purpose of this mechanism is to scare off predators and preserve the plankton colony.

THE OCEAN DEEP

Okay, now let's take a dive deep below the surface. There's probably no light down there, right? Wrong! Even though no surface light reaches here, 2 miles (3.2 kilometers) below the surface, this is where the most of our planet's bioluminescent animals live. The waters are as dark as midnight, but they're full of life *and* full of light. Keep an eye out for sea butterflies, swimming snails with lobes like tiny wings. Then there's the female anglerfish, who knows full well the power of light. She coaxes millions of glowing bacteria into her light organ, or *esca* (from the Latin word for "bait"), and dangles it in front of her large-toothed mouth. Innocent prey are attracted like moths to a porch light. The technique is very successful. Over 200 species of anglerfish are found in the deep sea.

Look! There's a stoplight loosejaw, a dragonfish with a loose, bony jaw that snaps shut like a mousetrap, eyeing us with its eerie red eyes like stoplights in the deep. And there goes a squid, changing its luminous colors and patterns on the fly. All of these creatures have learned to use their light-making abilities to survive, in many weird and wonderful ways.

Bioluminescent creatures come in many shapes and sizes, like this reef squid with its colorful luminous skin patterns.
ALEKSEI PERMIAKOV/GETTY IMAGES

A brittle star, a marine crustacean related to the sea star, stands out with its spiny, luminous tentacles on the floor of the Caribbean Sea.
JOHN A. ANDERSON/SHUTTERSTOCK.COM

2
SPOTLIGHT ON SURVIVAL

The sheer exuberance of fireflies is exhilarating, sprinkling light into the spring air after a cold, dark, barren winter. It looks like a lot of fun, but have you ever wondered why they flash? Why don't they just leave their lights on so they can see where they're going? Or maybe they are flashing their lights for another reason?

All animals need to do three basic things: eat, avoid being eaten and find mates. Bioluminescent organisms are no different. They use light to hunt, deceive their predators and find partners to reproduce.

An illumined abdomen is an excellent way to signal availability to potential mates. Light organs can be used to lure prey, create a cloak of invisibility, distract predators or even light up projectiles, such as luminous ink in bioluminescent squid.

BRIGHT LIGHTS: TINY TRACKERS

Luminous bacteria can be used as little light helpers for researchers to see how infections spread in living animals. Special cameras and microscopes are used to detect the bioluminescent bacteria. They can also be used to check for the presence of harmful germs in water and soil.

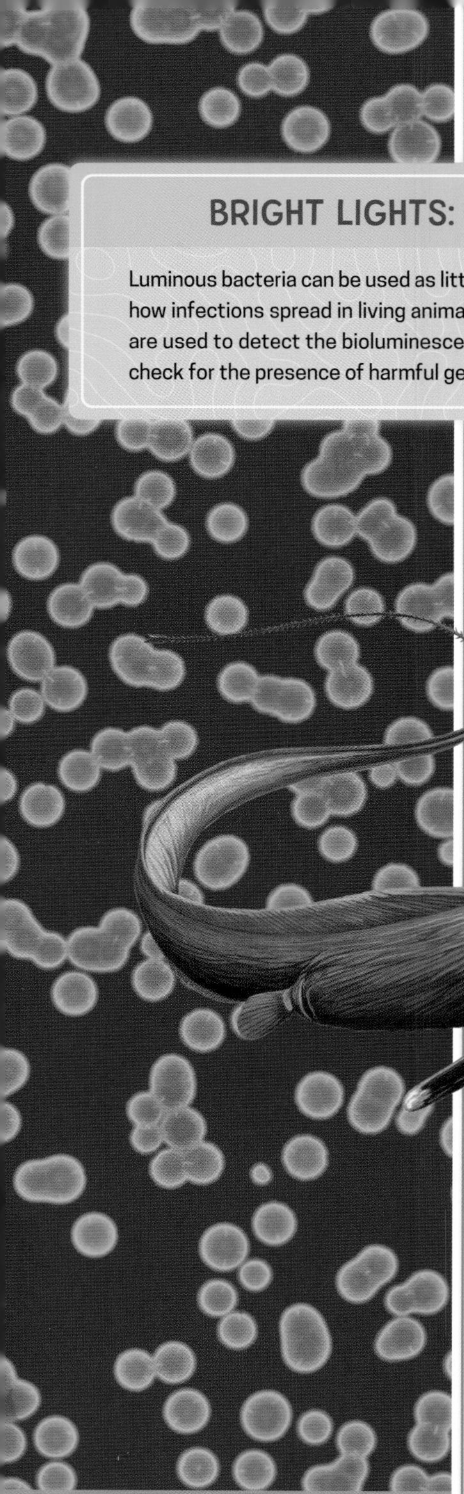

Bacteria, though tiny in size, play a big role in the world of bioluminescent animals. The light that bioluminescent bacteria produce is referred to as ***bacteriogenic*** light, and it is these bacteria that inhabit the light organs of marine animals in a partnership agreement known as ***symbiosis***. The power of these microorganisms lies in the collective light of their community.

Let's look at some of the other creative ways that bioluminescent animals use light to survive in their habitats.

This digital illustration shows a gulper eel, sometimes called a pelican eel, with its large mouth and long, luminous tail.
DORLING KINDERSLEY/GETTY IMAGES

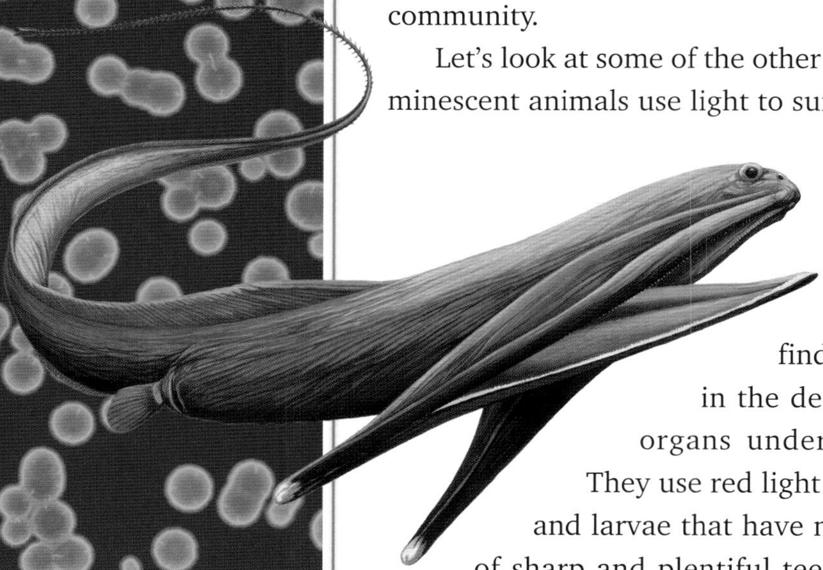

HUNT LIKE A DRAGON

Many bioluminescent organisms use light to find food. Dragonfish found in the deep ocean have red light organs under their glistening eyes. They use red light to hunt for small insects and larvae that have no red-light vision. Rows of sharp and plentiful teeth help these menacing creatures make quick work of their victims.

Other marine animals, such as the gulper eel and the anglerfish, know the value of a luminous lure. The gulper eel's glowing tail attracts fish like a fluorescent flag advertising an all-night diner. When prey swim up to have a look—*gulp!* They become the meal. Huge hinged jaws open wide to consume animals even bigger than the eel itself.

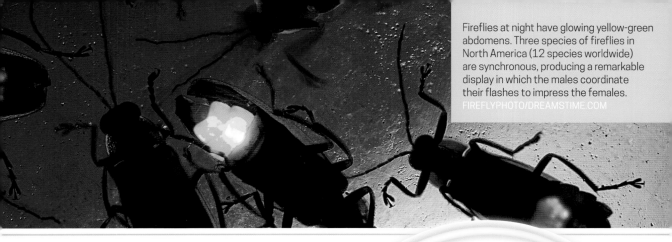

FLASH AND DASH

If a species can't reproduce, it will go extinct. Finding a mate is therefore a high priority for animals, and that task is a lot easier if you're sporting a shiny, glittering outfit. Male fireflies have very specific light dances to attract females of their own species. The females judge a male based on how he holds the beat (the flash sequence and timing), the acrobatics of his flight/dance and the brightness of his light. Wow, talk about performance pressure!

A male sea firefly swims toward the females while flashing in sequence. The flashes leave a stream of glowing pods in the water so an interested female can follow them. The females, sometimes known to wear glowing lipstick (but that's a whole other story), choose their mates based on the streams of light.

LIGHT AND WATER

Light travels differently through water than it does through air. It loses energy faster. Red light, which has a longer wavelength than some other colors (lower energy), gets absorbed quickly in water and therefore does not travel very far or deep. Some animals that want to see without being seen use red light as the color of choice since most marine organisms do not have red color receptors. A red fish will appear black in deep ocean waters. Blue light has a short wavelength (high energy), so it travels much farther underwater. Bioluminescent marine creatures that want to attract mates, or lure prey, or flash out communications, largely use blue light to do so.

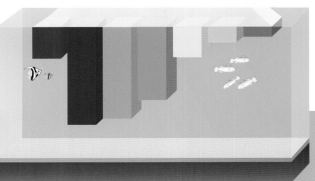

This illustration shows how sunlight is absorbed in clear seawater. High-energy blue light reaches the greatest depths. Red light is absorbed first. This phenomenon is responsible for ocean waters appearing blue to surface dwellers.
DESIGNUA/DREAMSTIME.COM

NORBERT WU/MINDEN PICTURES

CAMOUFLAGE

Counter-illumination is an important defense behavior that allows deep-sea creatures to hide from their predators. During the day sunlight streams into surface waters, making it look bright at the top. Marine animals reduce the contrast of their silhouettes against the lighter surface water by adjusting their light organs to emit just the right amount of light to match the brightness of the water above. Predators often lie in deeper waters, their eyes scanning the upper waters for prey. Animals that have matched their silhouettes to the light of the surface water therefore become invisible to them. Some squid are experts in this defense mechanism, able to change their light emissions so delicately that they can match the color and intensity of the moon throughout its changing cycle.

Counter-illumination is a useful tool and probably the most common use for bioluminescence in the mid-waters a few thousand feet (700–800 meters) below the surface. Marine animals dwelling here use light to stay hidden and safe in the dark ocean.

ODD COUPLES

The anglerfish has one of the strangest mating behaviors of any animal. The females are gigantic at three to four feet (about one meter) long compared to the tiny two- to three-inch (five- to eight-centimeter) males. After finding a female, the male bites into her side and connects to her bloodstream. He has no dorsal fin, no prey-attracting lure (like the female's esca, mentioned in the previous chapter), poorly developed jaws and a tiny digestive tract. In an unprecedented show of female dominance, she provides him with protection and nutrition in exchange for his sperm. Eventually the attached male loses his sight (along with his independence…because, frankly, he doesn't need it) and remains there for the rest of his life. Some females have been discovered with as many as six males attached to their bodies.

A RETCHING ESCAPE

Some marine animals, like the deep-sea shrimp, have a simple, no-nonsense plan. When in danger, vomit! Covering your predator with a luminous, blue-green slime is like putting a neon bull's-eye on its forehead in pitch-black waters. It's an effective way to get an opponent to stand down. It can also blind the predator temporarily, giving the shrimp a chance to make a hasty escape.

I remember unintentionally using the "retching escape" when I was seven years old. "You're not leaving this table until you eat your cauliflower, young man!" my mother warned me. But despite my best efforts, the cauliflower just wouldn't stay down, and I was allowed to make my own hasty escape.

BRIGHT LIGHTS: SURFACE LAMPS

In shallower water, the bristlemouth, a three-inch (eight-centimeter), densely toothed (bristly-mouthed) fish, uses two rows of light organs under its head and stomach to hide its silhouette.

A brittle star wraps its tentacles over a branching tube sponge in the Caribbean Sea.
DAMSEA/SHUTTERSTOCK.COM

ARMED WITH A GLOW

Brittle stars have learned how to avoid enemies by giving them a hand. A relative of the sea star, the brittle star typically has five flexible arms that it uses to crawl along the seafloor. The bioluminescent star (it gets its luminescent chemicals from its food) emits bright-green flashes from its arms that appear to scare off predators. This star buries itself in the sand near coral reefs, a couple of arms extended to catch prey. If a crab grabs an arm with its claws, the brittle star simply breaks off the appendage and makes a hasty retreat—leaving the crab holding a glowing broken arm.

BURGLAR ALARMS AND BOMBS

Many jellyfish light up when touched. This startle response is an effective defense against bullies. Hundreds of lights in the oval bulb of the jelly, the medusa, light up to frighten away the predator. Many other marine animals use light alarms to discourage predators from getting too close. The Atolla jellyfish is an alarm jelly. It flashes a blue light in defense when disturbed by a predator. Sometimes called the crown jelly, this jellyfish appears to wear a transparent

Luminous jellyfish float through ocean waters.
WEERAYUTWD/SHUTTERSTOCK.COM

crown. It is deep red in color, but it appears black in its midnight-zone habitat that no red light reaches.

The green bomber worm has evolved a unique way of defending itself. Living in the darkness of deep waters off the coasts of California and Oregon, this blind three-inch (eight-centimeter) worm carries a payload of eight bright-green bombs wrapped in a glowing sac. When it senses the presence of a hungry fish nearby, it drops its bombs. The predator immediately goes toward the bright bobbles, and the worm escapes as fast as it can using its paddle-shaped bristles.

MYSTERIES AND MORE

Brave ocean explorers with high-tech submersibles and advanced photographic devices are discovering marine animals that use light in remarkable ways to survive. Ocean explorer Edith Widder confessed to me that some biolumi-nescent organisms discovered in the deep are *so* strange that biologists have to guess what their light is used for (it's an educated guess, of course). Researchers were recently baffled by the discovery of a fish with pectoral fins modified into long, thin sticks. Perched on the ends of the fins, far, far away from the fish, were delicate little light organs that moved up and down with the current. Why so far away and so deli-cate? Maybe you'll be the one to figure *this* out someday. Despite all the different ways animals have evolved to use light, the basic light-making chem-istry they use is remarkably similar. Let's have a look at how they do it!

A young girl assembles a model of a molecular compound. Biologists and biochemists studied the mechanisms of bioluminescent creatures for decades before slowly unlocking some of their secrets.
GEORGIJEVIC/GETTY IMAGES

3
HOW TO MAKE SUNSHINE

Bioluminescence is of great interest because, despite its being part of complex biological systems, the light itself results from a single, very specific step in a biochemical reaction.

—from *Bioluminescence: Living Lights, Lights for Living,* by Thérèse Wilson and J. Woodland Hastings

How does a firefly light up its abdomen? What makes the light organs of most marine creatures shine? How does the gulper eel make its light so intense? We now know that special ***proteins*** need to be present for animals to make their own light. These molecules have been studied, their basic structures analyzed and their genetic codes uncovered. Many of these proteins can now be synthesized in a lab. Let's delve into a bit of basic chemistry.

THE DEETS ON DNA

DNA is like a cookbook. It's found in every living cell and has the recipes (the genes) that make the proteins that keep all the parts of living bodies working. We have about 10 trillion cells in our bodies, and each

In a DNA helix model, each nucleotide (A, C, G and T) has a specific color—red, yellow, blue or green—and their arrangement forms the genes that ultimately make the proteins.

cell has a nucleus, a special place that contains the DNA, which is made of smaller parts called nucleotides, kind of like the letters that make up words in a sentence. There are four nucleotides (A, C, G and T) that are the basic building blocks of DNA. Scientists can study the order of nucleotides (the genes) to figure out what instructions the DNA is giving the body.

BEETLE MUSH

More than 150 years ago, French scientist Raphaël Dubois decided to investigate how fireflies light up. He collected South American fireflies, separated their abdomens and made a smoothie of them (no, he did *not* drink it). He discovered two proteins (proteins are like the workers that keep the business of life running). The first protein was a light-making molecule that he called *luciferin* (loo-sih-fer-in), named from the Latin word *lucifer*, meaning "light-bearing." The other protein that helped produce light quickly and easily he called *luciferase* (loo-sif-er-ase). This was a type of protein known as an enzyme (enzymes typically end with the letters *ase*). Enzymes break down and no longer function when they are heated up.

Dubois noted that the protein luciferin could be used up, like the light from a battery-powered lamp. If the mush was heated, no light was produced, because the enzyme luciferase was damaged. Bioluminescent animals sometimes use slightly different proteins, but these principles of light making are pretty much the same.

HELP—FIREFLIES IN THE LAB

In the 1940s William D. McElroy, like Raphaël Dubois, saw the potential of fireflies to help understand how light is made in living things. But he needed a lot of them. So he asked for help from local schoolchildren (smart guy). Most kids were already collecting them just for the fun of seeing the beetles up close. McElroy gave them an added incentive—25

These fireflies have been collected in a glass jar for examination. Put a damp cloth in the jar to stop them from drying out if you attempt this, and don't forget to release them afterward. Young fireflies feed on nectar and pollen.
HUEPHOTOGRAPHY/GETTY IMAGES

cents (it was worth a lot more back then) for 100 fireflies, and a bonus of 10 dollars for the highest number collected that year (serious cash in 1940 dollars). He received 40,000 beetles in the first year. The numbers increased year by year, and by the 1960s he was getting annual collections of between 500,000 and a million fireflies. (I have to admit that hearing about these large numbers now makes the conservationist in me cringe. Many firefly habitats are threatened, and the populations of many species are threatened. Each living beetle is precious.)

William D. McElroy in front of a mountain of fireflies his young helpers collected. On the right the abdomens have been separated and placed in flasks ready to be crushed and turned into a liquid solution for analysis.
WERNER WOLFF, NEW YORK. SHERIDAN LIBRARIES, JOHNS HOPKINS UNIVERSITY

Lab assistants dried the insects and separated and crushed the abdomens, where the light is produced. McElroy determined that in addition to luciferin and luciferase, two other ingredients were needed to produce the firefly's light—oxygen and ATP (see the sidebar "Energy for Life"). Luciferin was synthesized (made in a lab) for the first time in 1961. Techniques were developed to gather large amounts of luciferase too, so that both proteins were made available for research and the development of other glowing products. Many fireflies were saved.

LIGHT FROM CRYSTALS

One organism that has been of major importance for understanding the chemistry of bioluminescence is the crystal jellyfish. Jellyfish are not actually fish. They are *invertebrates*, without any bones, hearts or brains and made largely of water. Trailing tentacles sting and paralyze prey, which get digested in the bell-shaped body of the jellyfish through a mouth that both ingests food and discards waste.

ENERGY FOR LIFE

Adenosine triphosphate are big words, so just remember the short version, ATP, and think "anytime power." Carbohydrates and fats store long-term energy, but ATP gives an immediate supply—like plugging into an electrical outlet. ATP is present in every living organism, providing energy to all the cells in the body. It's important for heat and nerve conduction, muscle contraction and most other processes that maintain life. Every cell in your body contains two billion—yes, two billion—ATP molecules. The fly walking across my computer screen, driving me nuts as I type this, uses ATP to power its wings and legs. On any given day, a normal person uses up half their body weight in ATP—that's how important it is!

bacteria

There are seven basic luciferin and luciferase molecules, identified by the names of the organisms that make them:

coelenterazine
(squid and jellyfish)

firefly

cypridina
(sea fireflies)

dinoflagellates
(plankton)

snail luciferin

earthworm

And they all need ATP.

There are pink, purple, blue, yellow and transparent jelly-fish, many of which are bioluminescent.

The crystal jellyfish is unique. It emits green light from hundreds of tiny light organs along the rim of its umbrella. It has attracted a lot of interest from biochemists. The crystal jellyfish produces a photoprotein (a protein that makes light) called *aequorin* that creates blue light in the presence of calcium. But didn't I say that they emit green light? Yes! That's because there is another protein in this jellyfish, **green fluorescent protein (GFP)**, that converts blue light into green light. A protein that can take blue light and change its wavelength to make it shine green is special

During World War II Japanese soldiers collected sea fireflies, a *crustacean* found in coastal waters off Japanese islands. They extracted a luminous blue paste by crushing the crustaceans with their hands and then smeared it on each other's backs. The blue glow helped the soldiers see each other without being seen by enemy forces as they marched in lines through the dense jungles at night. After the Allied forces dropped nuclear bombs on Nagasaki and Hiroshima, the war ended abruptly, leaving large supplies of unused crustaceans. These sparked some of the first studies in the chemistry of bioluminescence, both in Japan and the United States. That research led to a collaboration, the discovery of green fluorescent protein—and a Nobel Prize for three brilliant biochemists, Osamu Shimomura, Martin Chalfie and Roger Y. Tsien.

indeed. Patient study of GFP has contributed to several major scientific breakthroughs. In fact, GFP has started a "glowing genes revolution." Scientists can now use these photoproteins like flashlights to study activities inside the tiny cells of living organisms.

JELLYFISH JUICE AND GFP

It took one person's determination to prove that the crystal jellyfish had special light-making power. Osamu Shimomura, a Japanese-born scientist, collected more crystal jellyfish than anybody on Earth. He studied them for decades and decades. He and his assistants cut off thin strips around the umbrellas of the jellyfish, containing hundreds of light organs, and squeezed them through a fine cloth to get a luminous liquid called squeezate. Shimomura became an expert in how their light making functions. The protein responsible for the blue light, aequorin, had been discovered years before. Shimomura became obsessed with finding the answer to why the jellyfish glowed green. After years and years of patient study, he and his colleagues discovered GFP.

Sea fireflies produce sparkles and spew out a luminous blue liquid.
JONATHAN GALIONE/GETTY IMAGES

The common names of various types of jellyfish are very descriptive: moon jellies, crown jellies, red paper lantern jellies, cosmic jellies and blue button jellies, to name a few.
DBENITOSTOCK/GETTY IMAGES

4
OCEAN
LIGHTS

> **Imagine if you could go and explore a world you've never seen before, down in the depths of the deep sea...all around you are fireworks, brilliant flashes, glows and sparkles of sapphire, neon blue and blue-green sparks and what looks like puffs of blue smoke.**
>
> —Dr. Edith Widder

Oceans. They cover close to three-quarters of our planet's surface and are inhabited by creatures alien to most of us land dwellers. We often take for granted that the sun rises every morning and sets in the evening. It's different for marine creatures. Sunlight reaches only the top layers of water—the deeper you go, the darker it gets.

The ocean is the largest living space on Earth, often with no walls or places to hide. To avoid predators in the daytime, zooplankton, jellyfish, squid, shrimp and fish sink down to darker waters for protection. At night, every single night, they undertake the largest animal migration on Earth. It's not a movement across vast swaths of land. It's a vertical migration through layers and layers of ocean water, up to the surface.

OCEAN DEPTH

This graph shows the five main ocean zones, from the sunlight surface layer to a marine trench with a depth of over 36,000 feet (11,000 meters). The three most active zones are the sunlight, the twilight and the midnight.

Billions of ocean migrators rise to feed on plankton, krill and other surface-dwelling organisms. Then, as the first rays of morning light appear, the migrators descend again into the deep.

LAYERS OF LIGHT

The ocean is like a giant layered, transparent water sandwich. The top layer is the sunlight zone. It is full of light and plants like phytoplankton and algae, which are able to make food through photosynthesis. This layer is like the tomatoes and lettuce in the first layer of our sandwich. Animals such as colorful fish, sea turtles and dolphins,

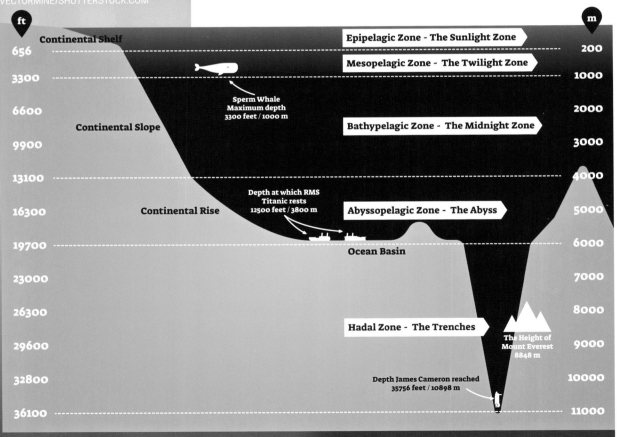

ft		m	
656	Continental Shelf	200	Epipelagic Zone - The Sunlight Zone
3300		1000	Mesopelagic Zone - The Twilight Zone
6600		2000	
9900	Continental Slope	3000	Bathypelagic Zone - The Midnight Zone
13100		4000	
16300	Continental Rise	5000	Abyssopelagic Zone - The Abyss
19700		6000	Ocean Basin
23000		7000	
26300		8000	
29600	Hadal Zone - The Trenches	9000	
32800		10000	
36100		11000	

Sperm Whale Maximum depth 3300 feet / 1000 m

Depth at which RMS Titanic rests 12500 feet / 3800 m

The Height of Mount Everest 8848 m

Depth James Cameron reached 35756 feet / 10898 m

which love the sunlight, live here too. The second layer, the twilight zone, is darker. It's the middle layer of the sandwich. There is still some light but not enough for photosynthesis to take place. Some animals, including squid and glowing fish, live in these waters. The midnight zone is like the bottom layer of the sandwich. No light reaches here at all. Most of the creatures that inhabit this layer make their own light. They are adapted to survive under the immense pressure of all that water (er...sandwich) above them. But it snows here continually—*marine snow*, that is. Bits of plants and animals are constantly drifting down from above, providing food for animals like octopuses. It's not white, fluffy snow—it's mostly poop and snot from sponges and other dead surface creatures. Yuck!

DEEPER WATERS BELOW

Few people have ever been below the midnight zone to the waters known as the abyss. It's one of the most mysterious places on Earth, yet a few animals, like the giant squid, like it well enough to live down there. The seabed in the abyss is a unique ecosystem in its own right. It is home to animals that have adapted to the extreme pressure and near-freezing temperatures to troll the different surfaces of the ocean bottom—animals like ghost sharks, sponges, eels and worms.

A few, like tube worms and some sea stars, have even adapted to survive in the trenches below the abyss. At these depths it's cold and dark, and the pressure is over 16,000 pounds per square inch (over 11,000 tons per square meter)—like the weight of a thousand blue whales piled onto your shoulders. That's a lot of pressure!

Organic particles, or "marine snow," descend into deeper ocean waters. Many are ingested by marine animals, but the mid-waters can sometimes look as if they're having a snowstorm.
FOTOGRAZIA/GETTY IMAGES

Let's take a little pressure off and head back up to the surface to take a look at the glowing surface waters.

THE MILKY SEAS MYSTERY

Over the centuries captains' ship logs have repeatedly recorded a strange, almost mystical phenomenon encountered on their long voyages. Picture this. It's the middle of the night and you're asleep on your cot in the middle of the ocean, rolling over wave after wave. Suddenly you wake up and stumble out onto the deck, and it's engulfed in light. The entire ship is suspended in a glowing glass bubble, lit from above and below. It lasts for hours upon hours, stretching into days. Then, as quickly as it appeared, it's gone.

Was this an alien visitation? A supernatural event? Few people on the planet have ever seen it, and science had

no explanation for it—until now. It is sometimes called a milky seas event because the luminous ocean water has a glow to it that makes it appear opaque and milklike. Clear skies appear black, but if there are clouds above, they become illuminated by the glowing waters. Samples taken by biologists during one of these events off the coast of Yemen more than 30 years ago showed high concentrations of bioluminescent bacteria attached to fragments of algae. With algae as a food source, the bacteria spread over a wide area of ocean water, as large as thousands of square miles. This occurrence is rare and can be found in remote Southeast Asian waters, so it escaped rigorous scientific study for many years. And this is not the only mass glowing event that takes place in the ocean. Sometimes they occur closer to coastlines.

A photographic rendition of a milky seas event. In 2019 a private yacht called *Ganesha* attained photos of what was described as a "luminous snowfield" off the coast of Java. Satellite data from 500 miles (800 kilometers) above confirmed the event.
DABARTI CGI/SHUTTERSTOCK.COM

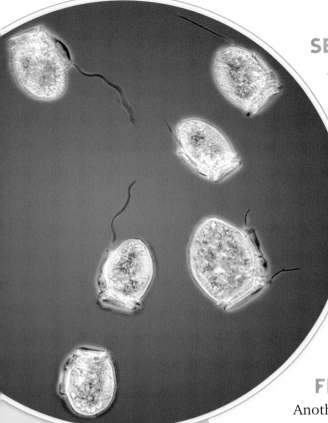

SEA SPARKLES

A bay full of sea sparkles, twinkling wave upon twinkling wave breaking on the shore, is one of nature's great light shows. Running your hand through the water is like dipping your fingers in liquid light. The microorganism that causes this phenomenon is a dinoflagellate, a type of phytoplankton with two whiplike tails. Many of the more than 2,000 species of dinoflagellates show characteristics of both plants and animals, and many of them produce light. What these tiny organisms lack in size, they gain in community, glowing together to light up the sea.

FIREFLIES OF THE SEA

Another sparkling coastal phenomenon is caused by a small glowing marine crustacean called an ostracod, the size of a grain of sand. Colonies of this creature live in seagrass beds and the sands of the North American Pacific coast and in the Caribbean. In Japan ostracods are known as sea fireflies—umi-hotaru in Japanese. They come out to feed at night and turn ocean waters into a sea of stars. The male ostracods, in an attempt to attract females, spew out luminous blue puffs one after another in an ascending line. But it only happens for an hour after sunset

A microscopic view of individual dinoflagellate cells with visible whiplike tails (flagellae). These tiny creatures, a form of plankton, live in colonies that emit a blue-green light in breaking waves or when disturbed by intruders.
MAPLE FERRYMAN/SHUTTERSTOCK.COM

BRIGHT LIGHTS: MICROBES IN THE SKY

New satellites with day-night sensors can detect glowing seas from space and keep track of these events around the globe. Research has shown that the milky seas phenomenon is the result of bacteria lighting up as one huge community when concentrations reach a critical level, a phenomenon known as quorum sensing. Interestingly, the number of bacteria it requires to create this phenomenon is close to the number of stars that we can see in the universe.

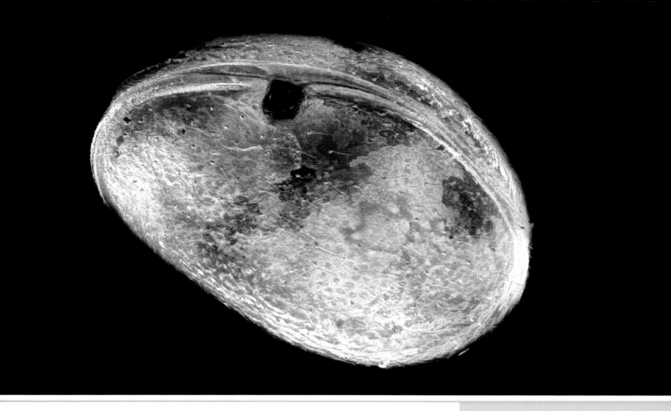

An ostracod is a bioluminescent shell-covered crustacean. One researcher described them as "a cross between a tiny crab and a spaceship." BLICKWINKEL/ALAMY STOCK PHOTO

and only on moonless nights—it's a natural wonder most people will never see. A rear-end reflector on the organism amplifies the luminous blue light produced by its chemistry. When it eats red algae, it is responsible for another coastal phenomenon known as a red tide, in which the waters turn an eerie reddish brown color. These blooms are often toxic to both marine animals and humans.

LOOKING BELOW THE SURFACE

For centuries the only samples we had of marine organisms living far below the surface were collected using inefficient and destructive nets that scraped along the seabed. The joke among marine biologists is that these nets captured only the slow, the dull and the stupid. Many gelatinous species like jellies were destroyed by the nets, making their identification almost impossible.

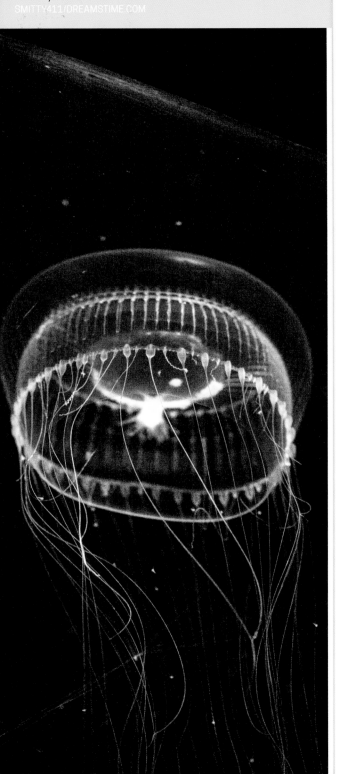

The crystal jellyfish, *Aequorea victoria*, with its 10-inch (25-centimeter) bell, has been called "the most influential bioluminescent marine organism." Its proteins are being studied for early detection of cancer.

To study natural behavior, it's important to observe animals in their habitat. Captured specimens are only helpful for studying their anatomy. To study animals on land, biologists often use "blinds," hiding spots where researchers can view the hunting, mating and other unique behaviors of their subject. There are no natural objects for marine biologists to crouch behind in deep ocean waters, no place to remain out of view. The water pressure increases as you dive deeper, so pressurized submarines are needed to explore the deep. It's a complex world down there. Bioluminescent marine animals use their light-making skills in remarkably diverse ways in order to survive.

THE STARTLERS

The **crystal jellyfish** (*Aequorea victoria*), introduced in the previous chapter, is 96 percent water, 3 percent protein and 1 percent mineral. But if you find one of these transparent creatures somewhere in the Pacific Ocean off the west coast of North America, give it a prod. More than a hundred light-producing organs will glow green on the rim of its bell, a response meant to startle a predator. Its radiant "don't touch" message can be seen a football field away. We learned how important the mechanism for making that green fluorescent light is. Some species of deep-sea shrimp also flash their light organs to startle and distract predators, enabling the shrimp to make a quick escape to safety.

COMB JELLIES

Tiny hairlike *cilia* move food toward the mouths of *comb jellies* and look a bit like miniature combs (that's how these creatures got their common name). These transparent **carnivores** can consume several times their body weight in a day, and they produce dazzling light shows that pulse through their transparent bodies in a rainbow of colors. Comb jellies are not actually jellyfish—they belong to their own ancient group, called Ctenophora. The ctenophores (teen-O-fors) have been living in the deep for more than 500 million years. Their bioluminescence comes from coelenterazine, a chemical they produce in their bodies. There are jellies, corals, brittle stars, squid and fish that all use this same chemical to power their light displays. But only the jellies, the copepods and the shrimp produce it—the remaining groups get it from their food, often made up of jellies, copepods and shrimp. Get the picture?

Comb jellyfish (of the phylum Ctenophora) have tiny hairs called cilia that move plankton toward their mouths, where they are trapped by specialized sticky cells. The colorful displays of light attract potential prey.

THE LURE OF BACTERIA

The *anglerfish* uses light to attract prey much like a fisher uses a shiny lure. The female of the species has a modified dorsal fin with a wire-like extension that ends in a tiny bulb of light. The glow in its esca comes from the light of millions of bioluminescent bacteria. The anglerfish attracts innocent prey to what appears to be a glowing morsel in front of the fish. Its massive spiked mouth is ever ready to gobble up its victims.

The *flashlight fish* also fills its photophores (light-producing organs) with luminous bacteria. Bean-shaped sacs under each eye serve as headlights for hunting. The back surface of each photophore is lined with crystal reflectors that help project the bacterial light. This clever fish can switch off its lights by rotating its light organs backward when they're not in use, like headlight covers on a car. This keeps the flashlight fish out of the spotlight when it's not hunting.

SQUID SWAGGER

The *Hawaiian bobtail squid* is a trendsetter in the ocean's mid-waters, sporting a patterned cloak that changes with its moods. After hatching off the Hawaiian coast, a young squid draws in bioluminescent bacteria as it swims along with its paddle-shaped fins. After a few hours trillions of micro light bulbs find their way into light organs in the squid's **mantle**, where they multiply and glow even more brightly in the safe, nutrient-rich environment. The young squid develops shutters, lenses, light detectors and reflectors. These enable it to adjust its glow to communicate, signal to potential mates and make itself invisible through counter-illumination, a method of protecting itself on its nightly vertical migrations to the surface and back. The

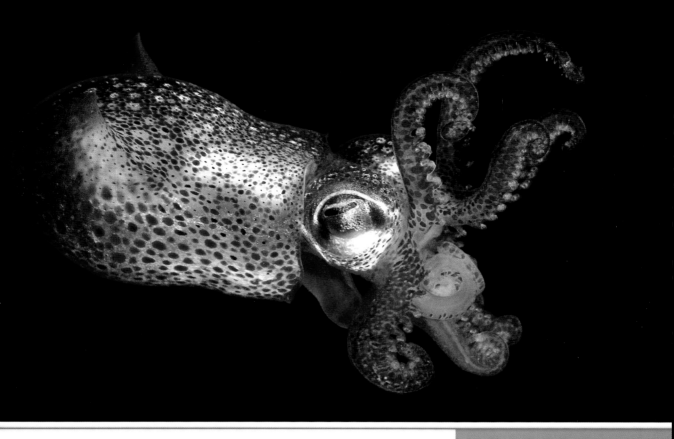

squid performs regular maintenance checks on its mantle lights, ejecting bacteria that aren't shining brightly enough and drawing in fresh ones.

During the day the squid sleeps buried in the sand, hiding from monk seals and lizard fish and gobbling up shrimp and crustaceans as they pass by. If a predator gets too close, the bobtail squid, like many of its squid relatives, releases a small ink-filled missile that encourages them to back off.

ODDBALLS

The *cock-eyed squid* is a bit of an oddball in the squid family. It has one huge, bulging eyeball directed upward and a smaller inset eye pointing down. The smaller eye is encircled by light organs that illuminate nearby prey.

Bobtail squid are tiny ambush predators less than 4 inches (10 centimeters) long. They hide in the sand to surprise their prey in shallow waters. Bioluminescent bacteria help them change the colors and patterns of their mantles.
_548901005677/GETTY IMAGES

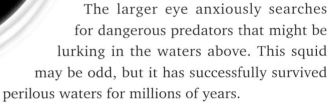

GARDENS IN THE DEEP

Deep-sea corals can survive as deep as 20,000 feet (6,000 meters) below the surface. Surface-level reef corals use fluorescent colors like sunscreen, for protection from damage by the UV light of the sun. Deep-sea corals are different. Their fluorescent proteins convert blue light to warm yellow/red light so that the microscopic algae that live in the corals can use the light for photosynthesis, providing energy to the coral. Most deep-sea corals are part of a group, called octocorals, that figured out how to glow early on in the evolutionary process. The group includes sea pens and bamboo corals. And look— there's a *sea cucumber*. It may look like an ugly lump lying on the seafloor, but when it lights up at night, well, it's a showstopper!

The larger eye anxiously searches for dangerous predators that might be lurking in the waters above. This squid may be odd, but it has successfully survived perilous waters for millions of years.

Then there's the *vampire squid.* It's been around since well before the dinosaurs. This squid earns its eerie name from its blood-red eyes and spiny tentacles (but it doesn't actually suck the blood of its victims like most vampires do). Light organs in its tentacles squirt a mess of glowing blue mucus to startle its predators and encourage them to back off. Paintball, anyone?

Speaking of vampires, the *saber-toothed vampire fish* is a fearsome creature. The long curved fangs on its lower jaw are so large that they have to slide into grooves outside its upper lip so as not to impale its brain. Lights inside the mouth make the huge fangs even more menacing, like shining a flashlight on your face from under your chin on Halloween.

As if this nightmare weren't scary enough, here comes a *dragonfish* with a mouth full of razor-like teeth. Red-light organs under its eyes act like close-range sniper scopes, and a dark-red body color makes the fish pretty well invisible in dark deep waters, allowing this monster to hunt without being seen—and dragonfish hunt in packs!

COLORED STRINGS AND GLOWING GLOBULES

The *rat-trap fish* has evolved a different skill to survive. Like a python, it can swallow food larger than itself by unhinging its upper and lower jaws. Under each eye it has a red, a yellow and a blue light organ for its colorful life in the deep. Marine biologists believe that the blue light is like the high beams on a car, allowing the fish to see into the distance, while the red light lets it see things up close. The yellow light's purpose is still a mystery. Any ideas?

Siphonophores are a sight to see floating through marine waters. Each one is a gelatinous, stringlike colony that can be more than 30 feet (10 meters) long, made up of segmented parts. The collective glow of their light has been known to illuminate nearby submarines so intensely that the sailors can read a book by the light. Some also release glowing globules in what appears to be defense by distraction.

Let's head to the surface and take a look at what's lighting up habitats on land.

The red-spotted siphonophore is a predator that drifts during the day but at night rises to the surface to catch its prey, unfolding its tentacles like a glowing red spider's web. This colony is in the Mediterranean Sea.
SEADAM/DREAMSTIME.COM

Fireflies prefer the humid environments of forests, wetlands, grasslands, parks and even backyards. Habitat loss is one of the leading threats to these magical creatures.
HTU/GETTY IMAGES

5
LUMINOUS LIFE ON LAND

*Sometimes, when I fear
the small light I bring
isn't big enough or bright
enough, I think of that night
on the beach years ago
when every step I took
in the cool wet sand turned
a glowing, iridescent blue...*

—FROM "BIOLUMINESCENCE,"
A POEM BY ROSEMERRY WAHTOLA TROMMER

Fireflies are by far the most well-known bioluminescent insects. Their twinkling lights have turned many meadows, grasslands, forests and backyards into magical places. Who hasn't held a firefly in cupped hands and marveled at the yellowish-green glow of cold light?

Visitors at night should be careful not to tread on the female fireflies that, in many species, dwell on the ground while carrying eggs. Firefly larvae live in damp soil and leaf litter, where they feed on other insects and snails.
JAMES JORDAN PHOTOGRAPHY/ GETTY IMAGES

Adult firefly beetles live for only a few weeks, so they waste no time in finding mates. Their favorite courtship hours are dusk and early evening, the males lighting up the air while the females remain either perched low on a plant or on the ground. A female keeps an eye out for a flashing male of her own species—the brighter, the better. Once she's spotted him, she starts up her own flashes, an invitation encoded in light.

Each firefly species has their own specially timed on-off flash patterns, called coda. The intensity of light varies between species. For example, the light from 6,000 females of a common European species is matched in intensity by only 40 females of a South American species. Wow! Now that's supercharged!

LAND-DWELLING LIGHT MAKERS

Terrestrial ecosystems are home to far fewer bioluminescent creatures than the ocean. Why? Total darkness on land is rare—the moon and stars provide enough light for

nocturnal animals to stay active at night. Also, on land there are many more hiding places to avoid predators—rocks, trees and other vegetation, caves and burrows. Animals that are active during the day have nests to settle into for protection at night. Why go to all the trouble of making your own light when you can just sleep until sunrise? Let the sun do the work! Still, some intriguing animals and even some plants on land have evolved the ability to produce light, including fireflies, earthworms, roundworms, millipedes and mushrooms.

ON-OFF BEETLES
AND THEIR MIMICS

Click beetles are closely related to fireflies. They get their name from the clicking sounds they make in their tropical habitats. When threatened this beetle falls on its back and plays dead. To right itself it bends forward, hooking a spine found on its upper body into a notch on its abdomen.

THE STICKY FUNGI EXPERIMENT

Foxfire is a term that refers to the glow of all the species of fungi that are bioluminescent. But they are pretty rare. There are only about a hundred luminous varieties out of an estimated three million mushroom species worldwide. Why some mushrooms glow is a question that had long puzzled scientists. Some Brazilian researchers put their noses to the ground to uncover the answer. Their study involved constructing sticky insect traps equipped with fake LED-lit fungi made of resin. The intensity of the glow was carefully matched to the light of luminous mushrooms in the wild. The traps were then placed on forest floors near other sticky resin fungi that did not glow. The data results showed that the beetles, bugs, flies and other insects caught in the glowing traps far outnumbered those in nonglowing traps. The scientists concluded that the bioluminescence attracted the insects. Since forest floors are often windless due to dense vegetation, the attracted insects also helped disperse the mushroom spores farther afield. Once again light making helps species survive.

BRIGHT LIGHTS: BAMBOO SHROOMS

Many fungi have a unique ability to digest lignin, a structural component of wood. That's why you'll often see small mushrooms on fallen trees and old stumps on forest floors. In 2020 an entirely new bioluminescent species was discovered on dead bamboo stalks in a community forest in the state of Meghalaya, India. The researchers were told that the local residents, including the Khasi people and the subtribes Pnar and Bhoi native to the West Jaintia Hills district, where the study took place, used the glowing stalks to navigate through dark forests at night.

The release of the spine propels the insect into the air and releases a loud clicking sound. Some click beetles are bioluminescent, sporting two brightly colored headlights in front, a signal of their toxicity to predators. Another light on their abdomens serves as an invitation to potential mates.

A glowing variety of cockroach that lives near a volcano in Mexico has learned to mimic the luminous click beetles. It isn't toxic, but the glow from bacteria that live on its *exoskeleton* makes it look toxic enough to deceive predators and keep them away.

ELECTRIC EARTHWORMS

A number of earthworm species, 33 in total, have figured out how to brighten up their underground burrows. Typically earthworms ooze mucus to help them move through soil, a natural and useful adaptation for organisms without legs that need to "worm" their way around. The mucus of some luminous species contains a shining secretion that often changes from blue to red as the worm ages and moves through its life stages. The glowing guck seems to alarm birds and other animals that feed on them. Not surprising—if my food started glowing, I wouldn't eat it either.

RADIANT ROUNDWORMS

Nematodes, also known as roundworms, are some of the most abundant animals on Earth. They are also very infectious and cause a lot of diseases. *Photorhabdus luminescens*, a luminous bacterium, lives inside nematodes, giving the roundworms a soft blue glow. The light attracts the larvae of beetles, moths and flies—but it's a fatal attraction. The parasitic nematodes invade insects and larvae, releasing the bacteria into its victim's bloodstream, killing it within days. The bacteria flourish with an abundant new nutrient supply while the nematode, also well nourished, thrives, producing hundreds of eggs and offspring.

But it's not always good times for the deadly duo. When food sources are low, the nematode turns on its partner in crime and devours the bacteria! Researchers are now studying the bacteria-nematode relationship in the hope of developing biological controls, natural ways to protect crops from disease.

During the American Civil War, at the Battle of Shiloh in 1862, injured soldiers who had been left out on the wet, muddy soil of the battlefield appeared to develop glowing wounds. This phenomenon has often been called Angel's Glow because bioluminescent bacteria that entered the wounds from the soil appeared to have protected the soldiers from deadly bacteria entering the wounded soldiers' bodies, thus saving their lives.

Some parasitic nematode worms are spread by blood-sucking insects. When the larvae mature in the lymph system, the adult worms can block vessels. The outcome is elephantiasis, an enormous swelling of body parts that causes many other severe symptoms.
KATERYNA KON/SCIENCE PHOTO LIBRARY/GETTY IMAGES

Fungus gnat larvae glow in Moria Gate Arch, New Zealand. The larvae flourish in high humidity, so caves, their preferred habitat, have become popular as tourist attractions. Light pollution has become a concern, as it can cause population decline.

MILLIPEDE MUCUS

There are over 12,000 species of millipedes, but only a few species are bioluminescent. Biologists are not sure why, but those ones are all found in the mountains of California. These multi-legged creatures remain buried in the soil during the day and wriggle out at night to nibble on plants. Their exoskeletons give off a "don't even think about it" glow. Would-be predators are treated to cyanide, a toxic poison, oozing from the millipedes' pores. I'll bet that's not the kind of late-night snack the predators were looking forward to.

BRIGHT LIGHTS: A SLOW GLOW

Snails are not known for their speed or their light. But in the tropical regions of Southeast Asia, there is a luminous species, about two inches (five to six centimeters) in length, that glows brighter when it is moving. It may be slow, but it is most certainly aglow.

IN FRESH WATER

The only known luminous freshwater organism is a limpet-like mollusk found in stony streams on the north island of New Zealand. When disturbed it emits a glowing slime as a defense mechanism against predators. Why are there no other bioluminescent organisms native to freshwater habitats? Total darkness is rare in lakes, ponds and rivers, since sunlight manages to filter into their relatively shallow waters. Lakes and ponds often have murky, cloudy water due to organic runoff from nearby land. Bioluminescent light cannot travel very far or be very effective in these conditions.

So these are some of the amazing bioluminescent organisms on land and in the sea that use their light-making powers in highly creative ways. Scientists are now using some of their discoveries about these powers to revolutionize the way biomedical research is conducted.

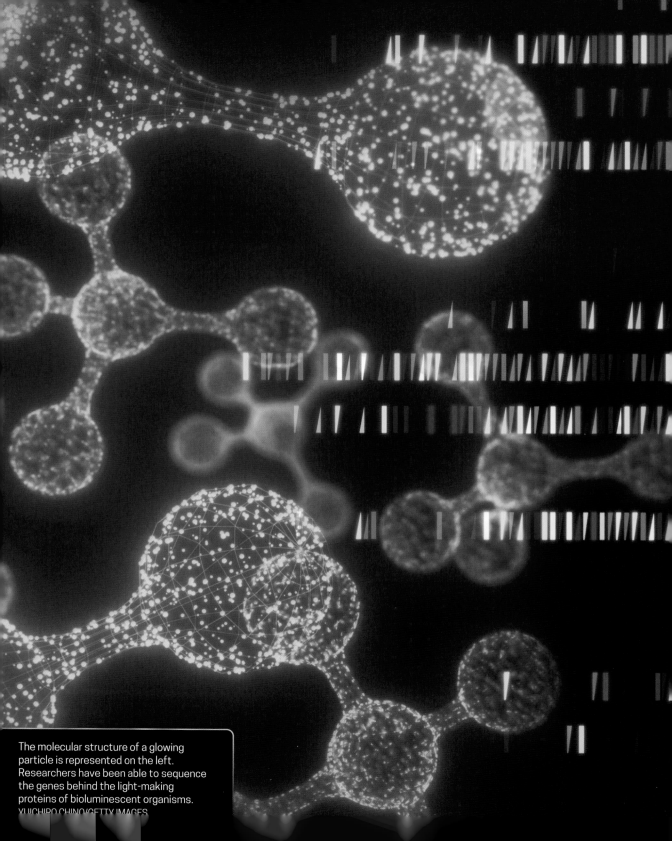

The molecular structure of a glowing particle is represented on the left. Researchers have been able to sequence the genes behind the light-making proteins of bioluminescent organisms.

6
ILLUMINATING RESEARCH

Who would have guessed that what was responsible for the green light in a jellyfish could change the way science is done?

—Marc Zimmer, author/chemist

When the microscope was first invented in the 17th century, it opened a window into a tiny world no one had ever seen. By unraveling the mysteries of bioluminescence, scientists now have a new research tool that allows them to look even deeper. The genes that make green fluorescent protein (GFP) enable researchers to follow molecules at the cellular level in living organisms. Researchers place these genes into specific proteins that can then be observed in real time as they move through cells, tissues, the bloodstream and organs. Molecules that emit light are easier to follow through special microscopes developed for this purpose. Glowing genes are now used in over three million experiments a year, and they are helping to reveal processes such as how cancer cells move in a body, which may eventually lead to new treatments.

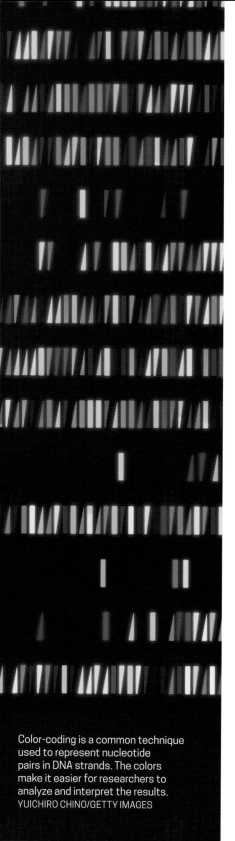

Color-coding is a common technique used to represent nucleotide pairs in DNA strands. The colors make it easier for researchers to analyze and interpret the results.
YUICHIRO CHINO/GETTY IMAGES

By tagging specific cells with GFP, medical researchers can study whether a new drug reaches and affects those cells.

COOKBOOKS AND SODA CANS

Once the recipe for GFP was determined from the genome, or DNA "cookbook," researchers were able to synthesize more of it. The genes for the protein were then inserted into bacteria to make more copies, a process known as cloning. The protein that makes light is shaped like a barrel with a light in the middle and is sometimes described as "a light inside a soda can."

Because of the light in the middle, GFP is a good "reporter gene"—it can indicate the location of the molecule it is attached to by glowing green. It's like attaching a tiny light bulb to the molecules or cells you want to follow. Multicolored fluorescent proteins have been developed from blue, cyan and yellow mutants and more recently expanded into the orange and red side of the color spectrum giving a broad palette of color. Now when scientists look at the cells under a special microscope, they can easily see the activities of each protein because it glows in a different color. It's like using different-colored markers to highlight different parts of a picture.

HELPING TO CURE DISEASES

EXPOSING CANCER

Cancer is a complex group of diseases that have something in common. The diseases create abnormal cells that keep growing and spreading. Then they enter and destroy normal tissue. Cancer is hard to detect until a lot of cancer cells have built up and reached a critical size. As they grow, many cancer cells mutate and become resistant to treatment drugs. The body's natural immune system that normally fights invaders no longer works on the cancer cells.

By attaching GFP to molecules in cancer cells, researchers are learning how tumor cells multiply and spread. Cancer cells in deep organs are particularly hard to detect because the light gets absorbed by all the structures in the body. A small surgical procedure in lab animals, a reversible skin flap, provides a window to the interior of the animal, and the illumined tumor and its development can be closely viewed in real time.

BRIGHT LIGHTS: TINY BUT POWERFUL

Proteins are tiny. Even electron microscopes are unable to see them. If the period at the end of the previous sentence were a cell (though a cell is actually much smaller than that), you would have to magnify it to a mile wide in order to see a protein in it. But now, simply by shining blue light on the subject with special microscopes, you can see proteins inside the cells. That's how powerful bioluminescence is.

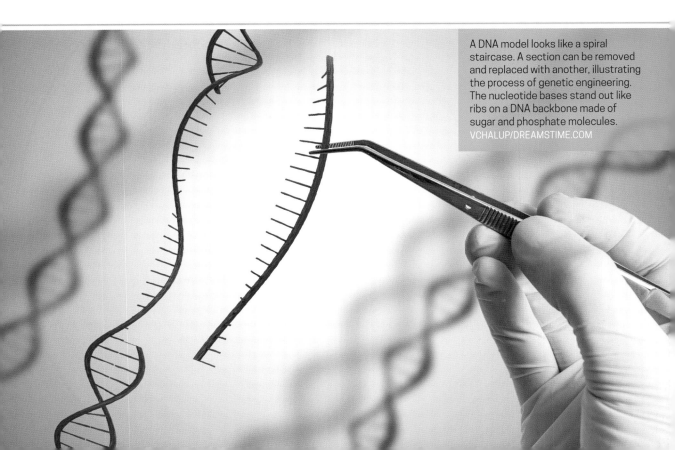

A DNA model looks like a spiral staircase. A section can be removed and replaced with another, illustrating the process of genetic engineering. The nucleotide bases stand out like ribs on a DNA backbone made of sugar and phosphate molecules.
VCHALUP/DREAMSTIME.COM

Biochemistry is fascinating, and now, thanks to bioluminescence, it is also rapidly changing. Biochemistry labs study the molecules of living organisms, the stuff of life. The discovery of fluorescent proteins is opening new windows into cells and organs.
BALANCEFORMCREATIVE/
SHUTTERSTOCK.COM

Recovery from cancer can be difficult. Chemotherapy treatments often result in patients losing their hair. However, new tools developed from fluorescent proteins are being used to stimulate hair follicles, helping to regrow hair more quickly.

THE KISSING DISEASE

They may sound like cute little insects, but "kissing bugs" bite and drink people's blood while they're sleeping. Found in Mexico, Central and South America these insects can lead to what is known as the "kissing bug disease" or Chagas disease. Infected bugs carry a parasite that they poop out near the bite site (they're bad-mannered too). When a person scratches the bite, the parasite enters their bloodstream. One out of 16 people in certain areas of South America are likely to be infected with Chagas disease, 10 to 18 million people globally. A third of those will die from heart failure and digestion-related complications. Researchers have now managed to modify the parasite so that it glows green. Using blue light and a fluorescent microscope, they can track and study the parasite as it multiplies and spreads. Understanding more about this disease could help save millions of lives.

DENGUE FEVER

Spread by the bite of a virus-infected *Aedes* mosquito, dengue fever kills one in five people who become infected with it. The disease is found in tropical and subtropical areas of the world, but it is migrating to other areas due to rising global temperatures (an outcome of the climate crisis). The female mosquito can lay eggs in a single drop of water, making it very difficult to control the spread of this mosquito species, especially in crowded cities. Researchers have genetically modified male *Aedes* mosquitoes so that their offspring die. They have tagged them with GFP so they can be tracked in the wild by their light. Wherever they go, they glow! The scientists intend to crowd out the fever-spreading species with the glowing variety that cannot reproduce, hoping that this will help end the spread of dengue fever.

The mosquito *Aedes aegypti* can spread dengue fever. Genetically modified with fluorescent proteins, luminous specimens are enabling scientists to track and predict the spread of the virus.
JAMES GATHANY/CDC/PUBLIC DOMAIN

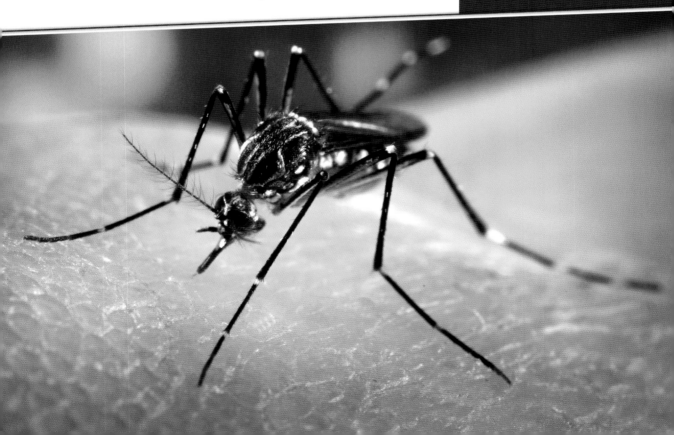

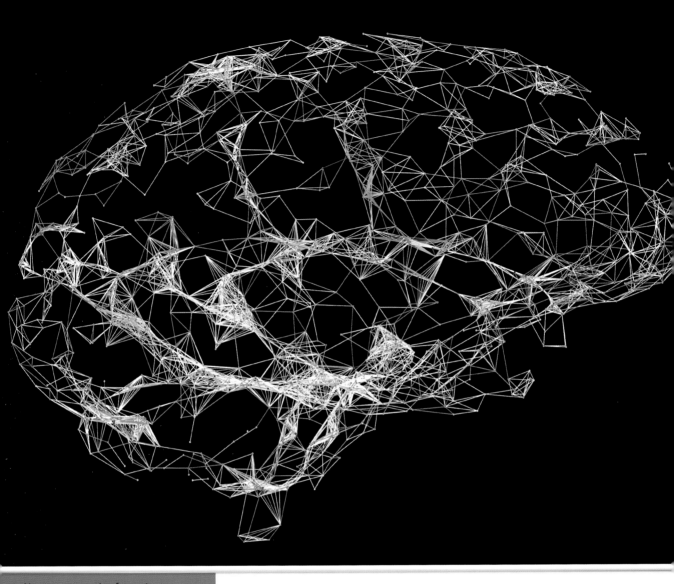

Neurons are made of proteins. Inserting different-colored fluorescent proteins into each individual neuron can help enable neuroscientists to unravel the complex networks of the brain to determine their function.
ALFRED PASIEKA/SCIENCE PHOTO LIBRARY/GETTY IMAGES

MALARIA AND OTHER DISEASES

Malaria is a tropical disease that kills close to a million people every year, many of them children. It is spread by a parasite carried by the *Anopheles* mosquito. How the parasite moves through a victim's body was not well understood until fluorescent proteins entered medical research. GFP allowed medical teams using special cameras to see exactly how, where and when the parasite moved through a mouse's body.

After infecting the liver, the parasite was seen entering the bloodstream and eventually infecting all the red blood cells in the mouse. Knowledge of these pathways can help scientists find ways to eliminate the parasite, or possibly the mosquitoes that carry it, and save hundreds of thousands of lives.

Influenza, SARS, COVID-19 and AIDS and other global diseases caused by viruses are now being studied using fluorescent protein techniques.

BRAINBOW MICE AND DISEASES OF THE BRAIN

Neuroscientists at Harvard University have modified mice in a project nicknamed Brainbow. In this study, the neurons and networks in the brains of the mice are made to glow in multiple colors. This enables the neuroscientists to follow each neuron through the tangled networks in a complex nervous system. Imagine if each of your friends glowed a different color and you were seated in a hot-air balloon well above your city. You could see exactly where each of your friends traveled throughout the day. Even if you had a hundred friends, if each was wearing a different glowing color, you would be able to follow them.

SAVING LIVES IN THE LAB

Modified fluorescent proteins provide an opportunity to minimize needless suffering and death in lab animals. They provide ways for researchers to see molecules moving through living organisms in real time, without having to kill and dissect the animals after the experiments to explore the results.

In the physiology lab, when I was studying biology, part of our curriculum was to study vertebrate nervous systems. For these studies suppliers collected stray dogs from the city's streets, and lab technicians drugged the animals to make them easier for students to handle. We were instructed to surgically expose the vagus nerve, the longest nerve in a dog, and poke it with electrodes to observe the response. I refused to do it—the dog was alive. I felt that even under *anesthesia* an animal would be traumatized by this procedure. I managed to pass the course without completing that particular lab assignment, but I switched my major to ecology at the end of the term. The inhumane treatment of lab animals has been an area of concern for me ever since. The use of modified proteins in research is providing hope for a more humane and compassionate approach to the use of animals in research.

The researchers are using this same color-coding principle to figure out how mice brains work. Touching a whisker on the face of the mouse with a probe, the researchers can see in real time which neurons in the brain are firing (lighting up). Unfortunately, at this point the researchers must cut the skull of the mouse and put in a tiny window (yikes!). Let's hope the imaging technique continues to develop so that the mice's brain functioning can be observed without them needing surgery.

TESTING FOR LIFE

The traditional method of checking for microbial life is to take a swab from any surface area and deposit it in a dish with nutrients to support life. If any microbes are present, the culture will start to grow. New developments using fluorescent proteins have created liquid solutions that when applied to surfaces result in glowing bioluminescent light if microbes are present.

Scientists searching for signs of life on other planets often focus on the presence of water or evidence of past water. NASA has discovered remnants of water on the Red Planet, rekindling the quest to find life on Mars. Both the American and European space agencies use fluorescent-protein test kits when preparing spacecraft for takeoff to make sure there are no microbes hitching a ride. It would be embarrassing to announce the discovery of extraterrestrial life only to find out later that it was carried on the space-ship from Earth. Such tests have also become useful in medicine for detecting bacterial infections. Some food and drink manufacturers are using them to ensure that the areas where their products are packaged are free of microorganisms that could contaminate the food or drinks.

RECIPES GONE WILD

When you're cooking in the kitchen and a recipe doesn't work, you can throw out the food. But that's not the case with genetically modified organisms (GMOs). They are useful for study in the lab or other controlled situations, but if engineered genes were to find their way into the wild, it would have negative consequences for ecosystems. For instance, researchers made a glowing rabbit by inserting GFP into its DNA. If that animal were to escape and pass on its traits to its wild relatives, how would that affect wild rabbits that mated with the glowing ones? How would it affect the ecosystem if all wild rabbits started glowing? Wolves and other carnivores that eat rabbits would be able to find them much more easily.

Many researchers believe the risks of doing this type of research are well worth taking. Why? Because these techniques have the potential to help eradicate diseases in humans. But it raises the question, To what extent are we willing to put our needs over the health of animals and the environment in which we live? Some people believe procedures that change the DNA of living organisms are morally wrong. Others feel that they are outright dangerous. What do you think? Is it okay to tinker with DNA, the recipe of life, if it cures human diseases? What if it helps feed the world's hungry?

Scientists have managed to make glowing plants by inserting the genes responsible for light-making proteins in bioluminescent mushrooms. Will this lead to glowing houseplants? There could be benefits. What about glowing trees planted to light up city streets?
BHAVESH JETHVA/GETTY IMAGES

PLANTS THAT GLOW

The beautiful colors found in flowers are the results of many floral pigments acting together. Getting them to glow is more difficult than it is with animals. However, an Italian scientist has succeeded in making glowing white daisies. If this can be achieved with other plant species, it's not hard to imagine a future where city trees light our way instead of energy-consuming streetlights, and where plants at the entrances to buildings and homes illuminate the path for people going into them late at night. Could this be a solution to the global energy crisis or a way of reducing fossil fuel consumption? Research is already underway on using luciferase to produce energy-efficient light bulbs. One day LEDs and fluorescent lights could be replaced with cold-light bulbs that don't require any electricity at all.

Glowing neon-colored fish called GloFish entered the market in the early 2000s as the first genetically engineered species to become commercially available. They have now escaped fish farms in Brazil and are thriving without predators in creeks and forest streams.
FUNSTARTS33/SHUTTERSTOCK.COM

COLORED MESSAGES

Scientists have modified potatoes to glow green when they need water. If bioluminescent proteins can be used on other crops, it could save millions in irrigation costs—especially important because fresh water is expected to become a limiting factor for food production as climate change progresses. World hunger is a real problem and will only get worse as global temperatures rise. At the time of writing this book, India, with more than 1.4 billion people, surpassed China as the most populated nation in the world. At current growth rates, the world population will reach 10 billion by 2050—that's a lot of mouths to feed.

Water is an important resource everywhere, and to be consumed it has to be clean. Again bioluminescent proteins are providing solutions.

PEARLS IN THE AQUARIUM

Researchers in Taiwan studying zebrafish organ development were surprised to find that when they inserted fluorescent protein genes into one fish, it resulted in the genes being passed on to the next generation. Commercial breeders picked up on this result, and now aquarium owners can buy Night Pearls, fluorescent zebrafish available in both red and green, along with glowing food. Sold with UV lights, the glowing zebrafish have quickly become popular. They are now available throughout North America (with the exception of California, which bans the sale of genetically modified pets). Since the zebrafish are not bred to be eaten, no national regulation agencies have the power (or will) to control their sale.

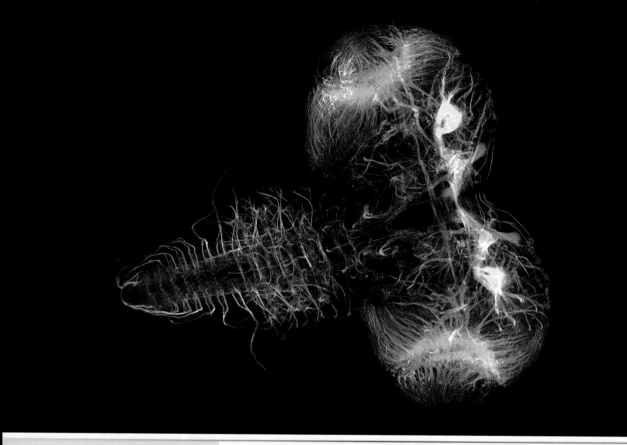

These are images of the brain of a fruit fly larva genetically modified with fluorescent proteins from a lobed brain coral. Spectral colors were applied according to position in the brain: red on the dorsal side, purple on the ventral side.
DR. WEN LU AND DR. GELFAND

They are being used to test for water pollutants. Fluorescent tadpoles have been engineered to glow green when heavy metal pollutants like cadmium and zinc are present in the water to which they are introduced. Luminous bacteria have also been developed that glow only when arsenic, a toxic substance, is present.

LIGHTING LAND MINES

War is devastating to the natural world. After conflicts end, land mines are often left behind in battle zones. These destructive devices are particularly dangerous for the local people who live in these areas. Modern land mines are increasingly made of plastic or wood, so standard metal detectors are no longer as useful for finding

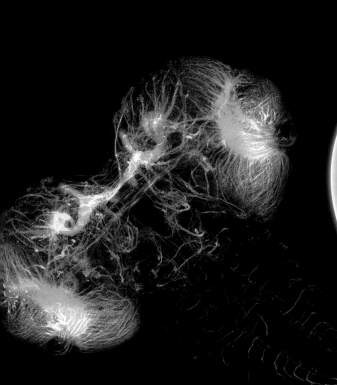

them. To address this issue, scientists are developing modified bioluminescent bacteria that light up when TNT, the explosive powder found in land mines, is detected in the soil. UV lights help illuminate the modified bacterial colonies when mines are present. Researchers are also developing plants that glow when TNT is present. The plants are much easier to see than the bacteria, but they have to be uprooted after the land mines are removed to prevent the GMOs from spreading into the wild.

BRIGHT LIGHTS: UNDER THE WAVES

A German submarine was torpedoed during World War I when the vessel accidentally entered bioluminescent waters. The glow of ocean waters had exposed its position to Allied forces. Defense departments have been interested in ocean bioluminescence ever since, funding many major research studies into which marine creatures glow and the secrets behind their bioluminescence.

Standing in the waters of a bioluminescent bay with the Milky Way streaming across the night sky is a life experience everyone should have. Sky glow from city lights has almost completely eliminated the view of the night sky for city dwellers.

7
SAVING THE LIGHT MAKERS

> Create experiences that leave you in awe, for these will be the highlights of your life.
>
> —Ryan Blair, American author and entrepreneur

One of the great challenges of our modern era is the climate crisis, which affects all life on Earth. The world's oceans have been working hard to keep the carbon cycle in balance by absorbing huge quantities of carbon dioxide (CO_2) from the atmosphere. But their ability to do so may well be reaching its limit. When CO_2 dissolves in ocean water, it forms a type of acid. Over the last century and a half, the chemistry of more than 300 million cubic miles (over a billion cubic kilometers) of seawater has been slowly changing. The acidic waters make it difficult for shell-building organisms, including coral, to build their homes—acidity corrodes their shells or slows the growth of new ones, thereby endangering populations. Many of these organisms are bioluminescent—and they may go extinct before we can even study them.

FLASH PROTECTION

Habitat loss is a huge threat to firefly populations. The grasslands, forests and meadows where they live are getting smaller, and many are disappearing altogether. For example, a rare Malaysian firefly known for flashing in unison is threatened because its mangrove habitats are being converted to palm oil plantations and aquaculture farms.

Fireflies rely on clear light signals to attract and communicate with mates. Light pollution interrupts their communication flashes. As cities grow larger, and *sky glow* gets brighter and spreads farther into wild ecosystems, firefly populations are struggling.

Another threat for fireflies, particularly around urban areas, is one that many insect species face—the use of pesticides and herbicides. These destructive chemicals, applied to "protect" agricultural crops and "protect" people from insects in urban areas, are particularly harmful to firefly larvae. Many people also question their impact on the health of human populations.

FIREFLY WATCH

Some conservation groups, like Massachusetts Audubon's Firefly Watch Project, work with help from citizen scientists to monitor local firefly populations. Supporters gather long-term data, monitor population declines and help determine what species are most at risk.

Fireflies are a popular tourist attraction, with close to a million people a year traveling to places where they can view the insects' aerial mating displays. Mexico has seen a rapid growth in firefly tourism over the last few years. India, Malaysia, Thailand and the United States are other popular destinations. However, a large influx of people brings its own dangers. Many female fireflies remain on or near the ground while communicating with mates, leaving them vulnerable to foot traffic. The IUCN SSC Firefly Specialist Group is busy educating firefly tourists, as well as guides and local communities, on how best to protect firefly populations. Well-intentioned tourists and locals also need to be told how to reduce light pollution from flashlights, vehicles, cell phones and security lights.

OCEAN LIGHTS

Bioluminescent marine species face a number of unique threats to their survival. Fishing boats interrupt ocean ecosystems with powerful lights. Dragnets scoop up marine animals in huge numbers, affecting many populations. Coral reefs that serve as nurseries for many fluorescent fish and other marine creatures are dying from bleaching due to warming waters. Coastal areas are being lost to fish farms and tourist resorts.

Young climbers descend through a beech forest on Montes de León in Spain to look for fireflies and other nocturnal insects.
POL DE LA CALLE BERNECHEA/ GETTY IMAGES

In addition to the acidification of ocean waters, an increasing influx of plastic and other forms of pollution affects the health of all sea creatures, including precious and rare bioluminescent marine animals.

HUNTING FOR TREASURE

Deep-sea mining, the hunt for precious metals—manganese, cobalt, nickel, copper, silver and gold—is proving particularly harmful to marine creatures, especially bioluminescent animals that rely on clear waters for communicating with light. Some of these metals lie in plain view on the seafloor, in rocky masses known as polymetallic nodules (a fancy word for a place that contains many valuable metals), and mining companies are racing to get the booty, potentially worth billions of dollars, by dredging the ocean floor. Follow-up studies show that seabed marine life sometimes has not recovered even 30 years after mining activities in the ocean have ended.

So why is deep-sea mining so harmful to ocean waters? Mining machines suck up metal-rich nodules the size of tennis balls through a pipeline that extends all the way to the ship on the surface. Once the metals are extracted, a toxin-rich puree is ejected back into the water, creating muddy, hazy waters and potentially harming filter-feeding organisms, from tiny worms to larger creatures like vampire squid and salps, which are gelatinous organisms that form chains as long as 30 feet (9 meters). These animals, most of them bioluminescent, feed on marine snow, consuming carbon and regulating the atmosphere. It is estimated that one mining ship releases enough dirty water in a single day to fill a fleet of tanker trucks 15 miles (close to 25 kilometers) long.

Drilling in the ocean causes not only sound pollution. Leaked oil poisons sea creatures and makes it harder for bioluminescent creatures to navigate and communicate.
CHAIN45154/GETTY IMAGES

Oil rigs installed in an oil field in the island waters off Scotland.
LEWIS MACKENZIE PHOTOGRAPHY/
GETTY IMAGES

The ejected material can travel hundreds of miles in the ocean, crossing protected zones, coral reefs and designated fishery areas. Without regulation of deep-sea mining, the health of ocean ecosystems will continue to deteriorate. Biologists are urging mining companies to develop a means of ejecting the puree as close to the seabed as possible in order to reduce the impact on water quality.

THE HIGH SEAS TREATY

Like deep-sea mining, oil and gas exploration can be very destructive to sensitive marine organisms. These operations use high-frequency seismic surveys to map the ocean floor, generating loud sounds that can be damaging to marine life. In addition, the decision-making process around regulation of exploration in the deep seas has not always been fair and equitable for all nations concerned. However, there is hope for the ocean waters. In Montreal, in late 2022, a landmark agreement was signed by 193 nations from around the world.

The High Seas Treaty was agreed upon to protect the two-thirds of the ocean that lies outside of national boundaries, known as the high seas. The treaty allows for the creation of more marine protected areas (MPAs) that will help conserve marine animals and plants. The agreement promises to share the benefits of marine genetic resources—animals and their DNA—more equally between nations. Small island nations rely on the oceans for food security since they have little land for agriculture. The ocean is an integral part of their cultural identity, yet decision-making regarding the regulation of ocean resources and their extraction are often controlled by those nations who will profit the most: Canada and the United States, as well as European and Asian countries.

SHOOT TO CONSERVE

I will probably never be seen in a deep-dive submersible vehicle—that's just not my thing. Perhaps it's not yours either, but thanks to intrepid oceanographers, photographers and videographers, we can still get a peek into life in the ocean depths. Many of their images appear in this book. On land a photographer can sit in one place for days, studying animal movement and behavior, waiting for the perfect shot. The difficulty with exploring and photographing ocean creatures is that the huge ocean waters extend miles deep and in all directions. Telephoto lenses do not capture clear photos underwater because water scatters light, so photographers need to get very

BRIGHT LIGHTS: DOWN IN THE TRENCHES

We don't know a lot about the marine trenches that extend below the seabed. The Mariana Trench in the western north Pacific Ocean near the Philippines is three times deeper than where the wreck of the *Titanic* lies. Only three people have ever been there. More people than that have landed on the moon. With ocean waters deteriorating, species in these remote habitats may be lost before we can even discover them, and some of those species could even contain cures to some of humanity's worst diseases.

close to their subjects and at the same time not disturb them. These photos are important for all of us to see, and for many of us they are the only way to get closer to the wondrous life of the deep ocean. Amateur and professional photographers alike are contributing in this way to the conservation effort.

MAKING ART WITH LIGHT

When I was a young, aspiring artist, I saw a photograph of the famous Spanish artist Pablo Picasso in *Life* magazine. In the image Picasso is drawing in the air—his canvas, in this case—using nothing but a small light bulb as a brush. He drew a centaur (a mythical creature that is half man and half horse) using just the bulb. The photo captured the split second the light image was still suspended in the air in front of the artist. The spontaneous act and creative genius of both the photographer and artist were contagious, and Picasso looked pleased with himself, sporting a rare smile.

Artists have long been fascinated by light. The Impressionists who painted at the turn of the 20th century, artists like Claude Monet (1840–1926) and Camille Pissarro (1830–1903), were not satisfied with painting realistic scenes. They tried to capture the light falling on their subjects by painting with short, vibrant strokes of color on canvas.

It was only a matter of time before contemporary artists were tempted to make art from bioluminescent organisms. The work of these artists is bringing more attention to the wonders of bioluminescence. What could

BRIGHT LIGHTS: FLASHY FASHION DESIGN

Beijing-based fashion designer Vega Wang is named after Vega, the brightest star in the northern constellation Lyra. She has long been fascinated by glowing jellyfish and other luminous bodies. The models for her Alpha Lyrae fashion show wore silk dresses printed with images of galaxies, constellations and nebulae and backlit by lightweight, flexible paper illuminated by an electrical charge. Multicolored glowstick fingernails completed the outfits and made for a runway show that garnered glowing reviews.

be more exciting than a luminous medium that is both alive *and* continues to grow and glow in front of the artist and the viewer?

Now some avant-garde artists are exploring the boundary between light, science and art.

Hunter Cole is a geneticist *and* an artist. She creates "living artworks." Her drawings with luminous bacteria grow and change as the microbes in her medium multiply. Recognized internationally, Cole's art includes paintings, photography, digital works and installations that highlight the beauty of luminescence. She teaches at Loyola University New Orleans, giving students the inspiration and know-how to create art while working in biology laboratories. (I wish that course had been around when I was at school.)

Shih Chieh Huang, a world-renowned artist, has long been fascinated with luminous sea creatures. While working as artist-in-residence at the Smithsonian Institution, he used light, sound, video and electronics to create an elaborate light exhibition called *The Bright Beneath*, an interpretation of life in the midnight zone of the ocean.

One of the functions of bioluminescence in nature is to attract a mate. This installation, titled *Angel Bride*, was photographed in bioluminescent light and shows a bride holding a bouquet of roses, surrounded by luminous bacteria drawn in the shape of rose flowers.
HUNTER COLE

Australian artist Peta Clancy created a series of human figures drawn on a surface of living bacteria for her exhibit *Visible Human Bodies*. The glowing/growing images, fed with multicolored nutrients, are placed in light boxes and illuminated from behind. The life-size artwork illustrates how much of the human body is made of living microbes, from inside our intestines and organs to the covering of our skin.

WHAT CAN *YOU* DO?

Ocean explorer Edith Widder says that one important thing young people can do to conserve bioluminescent species is to become citizen scientists. "If you want to learn to play the piano, you don't just study music theory—you practice and practice," she said. "Well, the same is true of science. You don't just study science facts. You need hands-on experience doing real science." Widder founded the Ocean Research & Conservation Association (ORCA) and serves as its chief executive officer. The registered charity relies on the collective strength of trained citizen scientists.

Here are some of the other things you can do to make a difference:

Raise awareness of bioluminescent organisms and the threats they face. The more people know about these amazing creatures, the more likely it is that conservation programs will be successful.

Light pollution threatens bioluminescent organisms everywhere, but firefly populations are particularly vulnerable. Artificial lights at night disrupt the beetles' mating behavior, as the insects determine when to flash based on how dark it is. Using motion detectors on outside lights can remove some of the light stress.

Light pollution is a problem for bioluminescent marine animals too. Sky glow from nearby cities can create surface water glow, exposing vertical migrators to their predators. You can do your part by reducing your night light footprint.

Pesticides, herbicides and habitat loss are also contributing to fewer numbers of fireflies. Encourage your family to eat organic, pesticide-free food and not use herbicides on front and back yards and gardens.

Plastic pollution is a huge threat for all ocean creatures, including those that make their own light. Single-use plastics like straws and throw-away containers ultimately end up in waterways and often find their way to the ocean. Once they start breaking down into microplastics, they can be even more dangerous, since they can then enter the bodies of marine animals. Use only recyclable plastics, and encourage others to use them as well.

If you live near the ocean, consider joining a beach cleanup. Not only will you be contributing to a better oceanfront experience for others, but you will be preventing more plastics from making their way into the bodies of marine organisms and impacting their populations.

Help support conservation groups by participating when you can. You may be surprised at how much you can learn at the same time.

An American horseshoe crab, collected from the waters off Tampa, Florida, is listed as a vulnerable species. These ancient creatures have survived for close to 500 million years but are now threatened by overharvesting and habitat loss.
CHENGUSF/DREAMSTIME.COM

MANY EYES IN THE SEA

Drawing inspiration from sea creatures like the stoplight loosejaw and the dragonfish, which emit red light that only they can see to illuminate their prey, Edith Widder developed a tool for observing sea creatures without having to catch them or scare them with a submersible. The system has an undersea camera that operates with red light and, to draw creatures to the camera, an "electronic jellyfish"—a circle of pulsing blue lights that mimics the jellyfish's burglar-alarm system. She called her creation the Eye-in-the-Sea. Testing her new creation from the observation deck of her submersible, Widder waited for four hours to allow the marine animals to settle into their natural behavior and get used to the presence of the new device. Then she turned on the red light to see what would happen. Within minutes a curious giant squid appeared on-screen, the first live video capture of this elusive creature. The Eye-in-the-Sea has since helped marine biologists discover many luminous species previously unknown to science.

Widder and her colleagues are now developing a new camera system to imitate bioluminescent displays, called the ANGLER. The new low-light invention is small and can float in mid-waters or dive as deep as 7,000 feet (2,000 meters). It is intended to be much more affordable, accessible and easily deployed for yacht owners or citizen-scientist

This stealth camera system called the Eye-in-the-Sea allows researchers in the Gulf of Mexico to watch and record the behavior of marine creatures in their natural habitat using red light that is largely invisible to them.
BIOLUMINESCENCE TEAM 2009, NOAA OCEAN EXPLORATION

A Johnson-Sea-Link submersible is lowered into the water by the Harbor Branch Oceanographic Institution on its way to the deep to deploy the Eye-in-the-Sea. It was originally conceived of in the 1960s by Edwin A. Link. BIOLUMINESCENCE TEAM 2009, NOAA OCEAN EXPLORATION

groups. The video footage of ocean organisms and associated data will provide researchers with many more eyes in the sea.

HANDLING THE GLOW

If you're not the type to dive into ocean water or run out into the field, there may be other opportunities to assist with research, lab experiments and engineering projects. New inventions will contribute to the sustainability of our luminous oceans and bioluminescent creatures and reveal more secrets hidden in these amazing creatures.

What could be more inspiring than animals, shackled by dark habitats, creating their own light out of nothing but their own body chemistry? We need to give them a helping hand to survive, not make it more difficult for them. There may be many undiscovered bioluminescent organisms with light-making chemicals that could help solve some of the great medical and biological puzzles of today.

GLOSSARY

abdomen—the part of a body that contains the stomach, bowels and other organs, or the end of an insect's body

aequorin—a protein found in crystal jellyfish (*Aequorea victoria*) that helps create their light display

anesthesia—the loss of pain and other sensations, achieved by an injection of drugs or use of gases before a surgical operation

bacteriogenic—caused by bacteria

bioluminescence—the emission of light from living things as the result of chemical reactions; sometimes referred to as cold light

carnivores—flesh-eating animals

chemiluminescence—light produced by chemical reactions

cilia—(plural of *cilium*) small eyelash-like hairs that often beat in waves

cold light—a characteristic of bioluminescence, in which less than 10 percent of the light generates thermal radiation or heat

counter-illumination—a method of active camouflage by marine animals, producing light to match their backgrounds both in color and brightness

crustaceans—marine invertebrates with a hard body covering, including crabs, lobsters, shrimp and barnacles

dinoflagellates—single-celled, algae-like organisms that float on the surface of ocean waters; some are bioluminescent

esca—a fleshy growth, typically luminous, that an anglerfish uses to lure its prey into close range

exoskeleton—the stiff external body covering that protects many invertebrates (animals without backbones)

fluorescence—a kind of luminescence that occurs when high-energy incoming light is reemitted as lower-energy light of a different color

fungi—(plural form of *fungus*) organisms that are not animals, plants or bacteria, such as rusts, yeasts, mildews, molds and mushrooms

green fluorescent protein (GFP)—a unique protein isolated from the crystal jellyfish that emits a green-colored glow under ultraviolet light

invertebrates—animals that lack a vertebral column (or backbone); about 95 percent of all living species are invertebrates

luciferase—an enzyme necessary to stimulate the chemical reaction in some luminescent organisms

luciferin—a group of chemicals that emit light when activated in a bioluminescent reaction

mantle—the main part of the body of a squid, containing all the organs

marine snow—a shower of organic matter, largely plankton, that falls from the upper waters to the deep ocean; also known as ocean dandruff

microbial—relating to microbes, very small organisms, especially bacteria, that can cause disease

mycelia—(plural of *mycelium*) the rootlike structures of fungi that look like tangled threads growing below the soil

ostracods—tiny luminous crustaceans that live in seagrass beds along coastal floors and often create sparkling coastal waters; also known as sea fireflies

photophores—light-producing organs

photosynthesis—the process green plants use to convert sunlight into their own food

proteins—long chains of amino acids, specific to each species, that are directly involved in the processes needed for living organisms to survive

sky glow—the glow of the night sky due to artificial light sources such as streetlights

symbiosis—a close physical relationship between two different organisms that is typically beneficial to both organisms

terrestrial—on the earth or dry land

RESOURCES

PRINT

Beck, W.H. *Glow: Animals with Their Own Night-Lights*. Houghton Mifflin Harcourt, 2016.

Davidson, Rose. *Glowing Animals*. National Geographic, 2019.

Harrison, David L. *After Dark: Poems about Nocturnal Animals*. Wordsong, 2020.

Keller, Shana. *Fly, Firefly!* Sleeping Bear Press, 2020.

Kuo, Julia. *Luminous: Living Things That Light Up the Night*. Greystone Kids, 2022.

Regan, Lisa. *Glow Down Deep: Amazing Creatures That Light Up*. Firefly Books, 2020.

Widder, Edith. *Below the Edge of Darkness: A Memoir of Exploring Light and Life in the Deep Sea*. Random House, 2021.

Widder, Edith. *The Bioluminescence Coloring Book*. Harbor Branch Oceanographic Institution, 2003.

Zimmer, Marc. *Bioluminescence: Nature and Science at Work*. Lerner Publishing Group, 2015.

ONLINE

Artist Eduardo Kac's website: ekac.org

Artist Hunter Cole's Instagram page: @huntercolephotography

The Bioluminescence Web Page, "Functions of Bioluminescence": biolum.eemb. ucsb.edu/functions.html

Green Fluorescent Protein: conncoll.edu/ccacad/zimmer/GFP-ww/GFP-1.htm

The Kids Should See This, *Swima bombiviridis* (Green Bomber Worms): thekidshouldseethis.com/post/31045041073

Monterey Bay Aquarium Research Institute, Citizen Science Using JellyWatch: mbari.org/lesson-plan/citizen-science-using-jellywatch

PBS Learning Media, Creatures of Light | How Biofluorescence Works: pbslearningmedia.org/resource/nvcol-sci-biofluore/ wgbh-nova-creatures-of-light-how-biofluorescence-works

Smithsonian Open Access images: si.edu/openaccess

DOCUMENTARIES

Bioluminescence on Camera. National Geographic YouTube channel.

The Blue Planet and *Blue Planet II*. BBC Earth YouTube channel.

Dive into the Deep Dark Ocean in a High-Tech Submersible! Greg Foot's YouTube channel.

The Making of "The Bright Beneath." Ocean Portal, Smithsonian Museum of Natural History.

ACKNOWLEDGMENTS

So many brilliant people have helped make this book possible. Thank you to Kirstie Hudson, Georgia Bradburne and designer Troy Cunningham at Orca for making this book shine. Special thanks to my agent, Stacey Kondla at The Rights Factory, for being the lodestar in my writing life.

To the inexhaustible Marc Zimmer, thank you for giving me the time for a personal interview, for checking the chemistry in this book and for your many inspiring books on the history and biochemistry of bioluminescence. My sincere gratitude to Edie Widder for taking the time to answer my queries and for sharing her passion for all things bioluminescent. Her book *Below the Edge of Darkness: A Memoir of Exploring Light and Life in the Deep Sea* is so eloquent and captivating that I couldn't put it down. To Rosemerry Wahtola Trommer, a sincere thank-you for the rights to use an excerpt from her inspiring poem "Bioluminescence."

Thank you, Hunter Cole, for sharing your unique photos and for enlightening so many young minds to the twilight zone between art and science. To my dearest Reta for walking on the path of light with me, and to all my friends for patiently listening to all the stories that I so excitedly shared.

Finally, to the light makers in our natural world, including young explorers, keep adding your brilliance to our living, glowing planet.

INDEX

Page numbers in **bold** *indicate an image caption.*

READ MORE
BY STEPHEN AITKEN

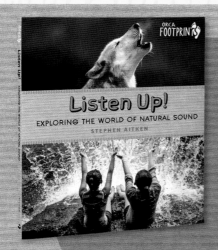

DISCOVER HOW TO LISTEN TO THE SOUNDS OF NATURE AND WHAT THEY CAN TELL US ABOUT THE HEALTH OF THE PLANET.

EXAMINE WHY DARKNESS IS IMPORTANT FOR PLANTS, ANIMALS AND PEOPLE, AND THE PRACTICAL THINGS WE CAN DO TO PROTECT THE NIGHT SKY FOR ALL ECOSYSTEMS ON THE PLANET.

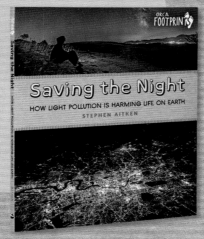

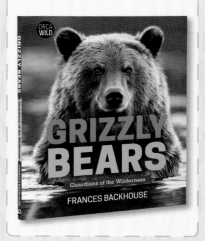

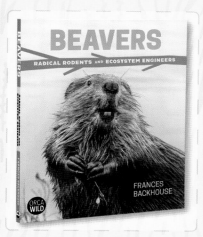

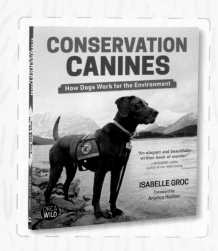

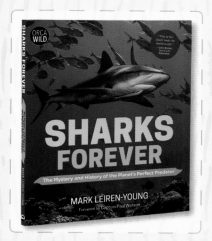

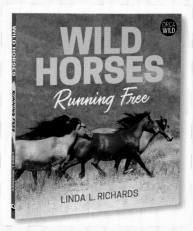

THE ORCA WILD SERIES travels over land, underwater and through the air to meet the animals who live in our world. The books challenge us to think about our relationships, both good and bad, with vulnerable species and habitats.

STEPHEN AITKEN is a biologist, artist and author. Despite an early brush with nyctophobia (fear of the dark), he became fascinated with bioluminescence while researching a book he wrote on the dangers of light pollution. Stephen's books fulfill (and sometimes feed) his longing to conserve the living creatures that share and enrich our planet. He has written and illustrated many picture books, chapter books and close to a dozen nonfiction books for middle-grade readers on topics including the climate crisis, the impact of artificial lighting on ecosystems (*Saving the Night*), the role of sound in conservation (*Listen Up!*) and other topics that encourage living in harmony with life on Earth. Stephen is the cofounder and executive secretary of Biodiversity Conservancy International, a registered Canadian charity, and is editorial director of the science journal *Biodiversity*, published in partnership with the Taylor & Francis Group. To see more of his books and art, please visit stephenaitken.com.

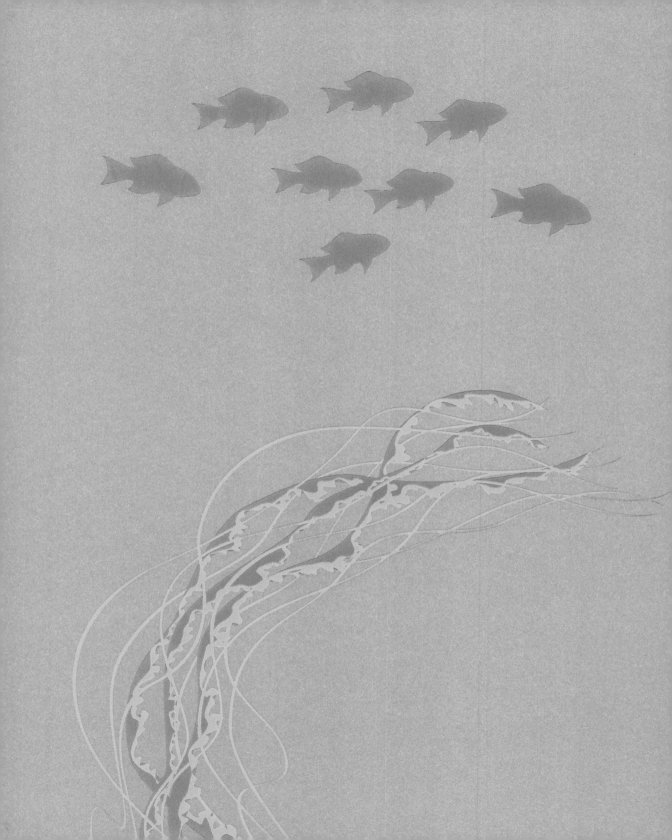